REFRAMING COMMUNITY PARTNERSHIPS IN EDUCATION

Reframing Community Partnerships in Education provides both the theoretical framework and a practical guide to engage educators in interdisciplinary, inter-organizational, multicultural, and multi-generational work to improve the social fabric of communities. Using case examples of best practice, this book explores transformational practices for community development, community building, and civic engagement. Featuring "Community Learning Exchange" pedagogies adaptable to a wide range of contexts, this book encourages educators—through use of participatory practices and a collective leadership model—to build stronger communities and advance learning for all.

Miguel A. Guajardo is Associate Professor in the Education and Community Leadership Program at Texas State University.

Francisco Guajardo is Professor and C. Bascom Slemp Endowed Chair in Education at the University of Texas, Rio Grande Valley.

Christopher Janson is Associate Professor of Leadership, School Counseling, and Sport Management at the University of North Florida.

Matthew Militello is the Wells Fargo Distinguished Professor in Educational Leadership at East Carolina University.

REFRAMING COMMUNITY PARTNERSHIPS IN EDUCATION

Uniting the Power of Place and Wisdom of People

Miguel A. Guajardo, Francisco Guajardo, Christopher Janson, and Matthew Militello

Routledge
Taylor & Francis Group
NEW YORK AND LONDON

First published 2016
by Routledge
711 Third Avenue, New York, NY 10017

and by Routledge
2 Park Square, Milton Park, Abingdon, Oxon, OX14 4RN

Routledge is an imprint of the Taylor & Francis Group, an informa business

© 2016 Taylor & Francis

The right of Miguel A. Guajardo, Francisco Guajardo, Christopher Janson, and Matthew Militello to be identified as authors of this work has been asserted by them in accordance with sections 77 and 78 of the Copyright, Designs and Patents Act 1988.

Library of Congress Cataloging-in-Publication Data
Guajardo, Miguel A.
  Reframing community partnerships in education : uniting the power of place and wisdom of people / Miguel A. Guajardo, Francisco Guajardo, Chris Janson, and Matthew Militello.
    pages cm
  Includes bibliographical references and index.
  1. Community Learning Exchange. 2. Community and school—United States. 3. Educational innovations—United States. I. Title.
  LC221.G83 2016
  371.19—dc23
  2015014476

ISBN: 978-1-138-84076-8 (hbk)
ISBN: 978-1-138-84077-5 (pbk)
ISBN: 978-1-315-73264-0 (ebk)

Typeset in Bembo
by Apex CoVantage, LLC

Printed and bound in the United States of America
by Edwards Brothers Malloy on sustainably sourced paper.

We are fathers, sons, husbands, brothers, friends, teachers, learners, and community members. Collectively, we are all deeply indebted to the W. K. Kellogg Foundation, the original Kellogg Leadership for Community Change sites, the host sites for the national Community Learning Exchanges, our university students, and all of the participants who inspire us. It is an honor to work with you in our Community Learning Exchanges, in our classrooms, communities, and nationally.

Individually, we would each like to share our personal dedications:

Matt: *I dedicate this book to my parents, Ronald Angelo Militello and Blanca Rosa Cárdenas—the creators of my first learning exchanges. Liz and I hope to be such for our four boys.*

Chris: *I dedicate this book to my parents, Bob and Cathie Janson; my wife, Mary Beth; and my sons, Dylan and Jack. Their involvement in the Community Learning Exchange has brought even greater joy to the work.*

Miguel and Francisco: *We dedicate this book to our parents, our brothers, our extended family, and the community that raised us. They helped us shape our meaning and process of community.*

We would also like to thank our National Community Learning Exchange Team and W.K. Kellogg Foundation partners:

Maenette Benham
Cheryl Fields
Lee Francis
Emiliano Guajardo
Valerie Johnson
Sophie Maxis
Dominic Militello
Dale Nienow
John Oliver
Kwesi Rollins
Karma Ruder
Steve Stapleton
Frank Taylor
Lynda Tredway
Mónica Valadez

You have been our brothers and sisters in this very important work. We look forward to the next iterations of this journey with you.

MAKING IT LAST (A MUSTARD SEED PANTOUM)

By Lee Francis

There are gardens everywhere we look and they are green and they are
golden.
We must be careful to let them tangle and twist in the sunshine
unafraid to step into the unknown stories that wrap around each leaf
and stem
and unafraid of hard times, always unfinished, always reaching to the sky.

We must be careful to let them tangle and twist in the sunshine
these mustard seeds. They will grow tall and joyous from strong soil
and unafraid of hard times. Always unfinished and always reaching to the sky,
they will blossom and grow in ways we are not even able to imagine.

These mustard seeds. They will grow tall and joyous. From strong soil,
they emerge with prayers on their leaves which we will eat and form
stories;
they will blossom and grow in ways we are not even able to imagine
from months ago when we first pressed our hands into the earth.

They emerge. With prayers on their leaves (which we will eat and form
stories)
these ancient plant dreams remind us that we are also mustard seeds
from months ago when we first pressed our hands into the earth
and began a journey of growing. And now we understand:

these ancient plant dreams remind us that we are also mustard seeds
unafraid to step into the unknown stories, that wrap around each leaf
and stem,
and begin a journey of growing. And now we understand
there are gardens everywhere we look and they are green. And they are
golden.

See Video Links in 'Additional Resources' to view Lee reading this poem.

CONTENTS

FOREWORD

When I was a little girl, I often found myself sitting on my grandmother's *pūne'e* (portable couch) in the evenings, listening to stories; we didn't have a television or a radio. My grandparents shared all sorts of stories, from ancient Hawaiian myths to contemporary tales to stories of everyday living. There were stories of grand journeys, of sorrow and joy, of heroes and villains and tricksters—stories that tapped into deep reservoirs of human experience and ancestral knowledge that shape generation after generation. The perpetuity of the telling and retelling of these well-crafted stories is our interface with our genealogy and uniquely bonds us to everything that surrounds us. I cannot actually recall when the instructional messages of these stories my grandparents shared began to show up in my work. But they did, and I am grateful.

What I do recall is that the storytelling and my need to share my grandparents' stories became an important foundation for my work as a scholar and teacher. That passion found a kindred spirit in Dr. Valorie Johnson, the program director for the W.K. Kellogg Foundation's Kellogg Leadership for Community Change (KLCC) initiative, the seed for the work of this book. The fact that we found kindred warrior spirits in mid-Michigan was remarkable! Even more, working in thought-provoking, community-based, collective change initiatives with a team of community advocates, scholars, and teachers—the authors of this book—is an honor, and the incredible adventure that this book describes!

The story of this book invites the reader to go to his or her source, to go to that place that is the pool of knowledge that defines "how" we walk, learn, and live in this world. For myself, it is best stated in an *'ōlelo no'eau* (Native Hawaiian wise saying) that my grandparents often used: *I ulu nō ka lā'au i ke kumu!* (Learning from those that have come before us!). Indeed, when we listen to the guiding principles shared in the ancestral stories of our homeland, of our families, boundaries and blinders melt away, and we can envision where we need to be. It is that source, that unique genealogical center of our ontological worldview, which reminds us of our value principles and reconnects us with a myriad of relations that enrich and strengthen our mission to drive collective action and actualize powerful, transformational impact.

Beginning in a place of vibrant knowledge and relations found in the stories of place and people—a central "idea" of this book—leads the reader/learner to a sort of *'auwai* (a canal that transports precious water). This pedagogical pathway invites engagement, gratefulness and graciousness, inclusivity and innovation, critical voice, and collectivity. The learning processes presented in this text strengthen each person's core of integrity and then lovingly unite the truths of this new politic into a powerful collective whole that is empowered to *E kūlia i ka nu'u kākou a pau!* (We must, together, strive for the summit!). While this work speaks to the strength of human spirit, it is also quite pragmatic. The pedagogies presented in the text teach how we come together to apply our knowledge and skills to make a difference in the lives of the people we love and care about. Strategies teach us how to move toward cross-sector convergence, in which barriers between traditional sectors (business, government, and non-governmental organizations, or NGOs) are not just blurred but redefined. In this manner, we learn to address complex problems both pragmatically and innovatively in an interdisciplinary, intergenerational, multicultural, and intra-/inter-organizational manner. Through these processes, people and organizations, both internally and externally, redefine their social purpose, and it is that vision of justice that drives action. It is our collective work that drives us to achieve the summit.

The context of this book is bold, inviting, and inspirational. The authors' stories coupled with the technicalities and "rhythm" of the work call on us to develop a collective public voice for justice and equity that is grounded in our *mo'okūauhau* (genealogy of place, people, and relations) and in the richness of our contemporary community knowledge and voice, a space and place where the stories of struggles inspire. I am a strong believer that we each come to this "work" when we are called to it—if you are reading this book, then you have been called.

The work, as it is described in this book, is a pathway for how we express the quintessential quality of humanity, *Ulu a'e ke welina a ke aloha!* (Loving the abundance of all that nurtures is the practice of an awake/aware and open mind!).

Maenette K.P. Ah Nee–Benham, Dean Hawai'inuiākea
School of Hawaiian Knowledge, University of Hawai'i at Mānoa

PREFACE

This book is for educators who dare to do things differently. It is an invitation to engage in a series of innovative teaching, learning, and service processes that employ life-changing pedagogical practices for the purpose of engaging local community members as agents who give shape to the schools, organizations, and communities in which they work and live. The story of the Community Learning Exchange challenges us to disrupt the practice of sitting in rows, of rote memorization, of doing the questions in the back of the chapter, and of obligatory homework. This story is counter to all that, as it tells narratives of students, teachers, parents, and community members teaching and learning in a community context. The lessons are learned through robust relationship building—through careful examination of the strengths and assets of communities, and through exploring the narrative and history of the community. The lessons begin with the self, as students and community members involved in the process are challenged to understand their personal stories before they delve into stories of organizations and community. The emerging theory that makes sense of the Community Learning Exchange is fundamentally rooted in the goodness of people. It encourages participants to solve their own problems as they look to their own gifts and the values of the community for solutions.

How to Use the Book

There is an inherent implication that authors are experts. In this journey we pose more questions than answers. We invite the reader to author his or her personal, organizational, and community narratives, and we expect this process can be the beginning of an important conversation. This book is a journey of critical self-reflection and purposefully encourages conversations with families, organizations, and communities.

The book is divided into four parts. Part I, "The Ideas Behind the Action," begins with Chapter 1, "The Community Learning Exchange," a description of a Community Learning Exchange (CLE), which includes the history, purpose, and genealogy of a CLE. Chapter 2, "Meaning Making, Axioms, and Ecologies for Engagement," provides the theoretical underpinnings of this work. Finally, Chapter 3, "A Theory of Change in Action," explores how to move this work from theory to practice.

Part II, "The Work" includes specific stories to illustrate what the work of the Community Learning Exchange looks like. Chapter 4, "Storytelling: Stories of Impact," uses stories, including first person accounts, of the work of CLEs. Chapter 5, "Storytelling: Making Sense of the Lived Experiences," lays the theories from Part I as an analytical tool to understand the stories.

Part III, "Dynamic-Critical Pedagogies," provides specific teaching and learning strategies. These represent a set of social technologies that we have embedded into our teaching and learning. We begin with Chapter 6, "Teaching for Learning, Learning to Teach," to ground the intentionality of the work. Chapter 7, "Dynamic-Critical Pedagogies of Reflection," and Chapter 8, "Dynamic-Critical Pedagogies with and in Community," provide the procedural, or *how-to*, elements of the CLE work. The pedagogies are defined, and examples of their implementation are provided. These pedagogies are meant to be lived, to be changed and adapted by users to meet the specific needs of their organizations and communities.

Part IV, "Impacts, Reflections, and an Invitation to Action," brings the book home. Chapter 9, "Impacts From and Reflections on the CLE Work," offers an account of how others use this work in their professional practice. This chapter also provides space to reflect on our work with CLEs and revisits the ecologies of knowing: self, organization, and community. Chapter 10, "Conclusion and an Invitation to Action," challenges readers to engage in the work of the Community Learning Exchange.

The *Appendix* provides additional background information about Community Learning Exchanges, such as concrete examples of agendas and themes and various forms of Community Learning Exchanges. *Video and Web Links* provide examples of the CLE work in action as well as resources that may be of further assistance. We conclude with a bibliography of *Readings* that have expanded our imagination as activist scholars, including a set of seminal readings that has informed the work that led to the creation of this book. The reader will find publications that have emerged from our own development and understanding of the work in private and public spaces.

Invitation

The book is designed to read straight through as a traditional text, but it can also be visited and revisited at various places—just as we enter this endeavor at various places of development and at different times in our lives, and as we work together to address different issues in different communities. The book is *axiomatic* and can be read as a starting point for learning about this work and the ideas behind it, from the beginning straight through to the end. We believe the truth in the work of the Community Learning Exchange will also be experienced by readings of this book guided by the distinct and unique needs of readers who bring with them their own learning styles and varied contexts with families, organizations, and communities.

Finally, we hope this book will be *read in community*. Very much in the spirit of those we document and explore within it, this book came to life through a collective process. Just as we have brought the lessons of the Community Learning Exchange back to our families, our neighbors, our colleagues, and our communities, we hope that you bring this message to those in your homes, organizations, and communities. As a result, we invite the reader to use www.community learningexchange.org/ and www.facebook.com/communitylearningexchange, which are designed to provide resources and to continue the conversations we hope the work provokes.

This book was written in friendship, and we hope it will be read in that spirit. We encourage you to consider a few meta-questions as you read:

- What stories do you need to explore about yourself, your organization, and your community?
- Who do you need to talk with to reflect on this book?
- Who else do you feel needs to read this book?
- What is your plan of action? What are the principles (axioms), theory of change (RASPPA), and strategies (critical-dynamic pedagogies)?

The CLE experience ignites the imagination of participants and pushes them to engage in teaching, learning, leadership, and community development in ways that are historically appropriate and culturally respectful. We invite you to join us in exploring the imagination.

PART I
The Ideas Behind the Action

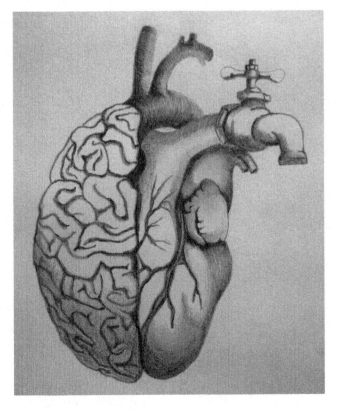

DRAWING 1 Artwork by Mónica Valadez.

Source: Mónica Valadez. Used with permission.

1

THE COMMUNITY LEARNING
EXCHANGE

This book is about a process and a way of life that celebrate the power of place
and the wisdom of people. A Community Learning Exchange (CLE) provides
an opportunity for diverse community members—leaders, activists, educators,
youth, elders—to come together for a period of engaged, deep learning. Together
in relationship, these community members openly examine their common challenges, collective gifts, and then freely exchange successful approaches and tools
that can drive changes within themselves, their organizations (including schools),
and their communities. CLEs break the isolation people working toward organizational and community change often feel by encouraging the deepening of
their relationships with others. CLEs provide time and space for everyday people
to come together and join in deep and purposeful conversations that are very
difficult to have within the blur of our hectic daily schedules and lives. During
CLEs, participants work to establish conditions of safety and trust so that they
can openly share their gifts with others so that together they can challenge themselves, their organizations, and their communities in order to better meet their
individual and collective needs while supporting the development, growth, and
happiness of others in equitable and just ways.

This book is born out of the gifts and strengths we have seen in communities.
It is nurtured by the need to *reframe school and community partnerships*. We can see
inefficiencies in our bureaucracies, inequities in our communities, and injustices
in our organizations and institutions. But how can we change them? How do
we go about transforming those very things that mediate individuals and society
so that we can make life healthier and more fulfilling for ourselves and for others. Some of us want to help reform schools that do not seem to be effectively
nurturing our sons' and daughters' growth and development. Others are looking

to make our neighborhoods safer. Still others recognize the challenges newcomers face in our cities. We believe that the Community Learning Exchange and its foundational axioms provide a tried, tested, and true pathway to those changes and transformations. Specifically, individual, collective, and community changes occur through Community Learning Exchanges built from the axioms that (a) learning and leadership are a dynamic social process, (b) conversations are critical and central pedagogies, (c) the people closest to the issues are best situated to discover answers to local questions and problems, (d) crossing boundaries enriches how we develop and learn, and (e) hope and change are built on assets and dreams of locals and their communities.

We also know that organizational and community changes are complex processes and that complexity requires that we seek to understand them in intentional ways. Organizations and communities contain an ever-changing array of people with diverse needs and concerns, and assets and gifts. These complex dynamics require that we are purposeful in our efforts to understand them. Over time and across settings and communities, the Community Learning Exchange has produced and informed a theory for how those changes occur, and thus how they can be nurtured and directed. If the five axioms of the Community Learning Exchange provide postulates that enrich and deepen meaning with each application, the Community Learning Exchange theory of change provides a template or a lens through which we both examine and enact changes in our organizations and communities. Specifically, the CLE theory of change invites us to look at our families, our neighborhoods, our communities, and our organizations with an eye for relationships, assets, stories, place, politic, and action (RASPPA). Importantly, the RASPPA theory of change creates the cognitive, affective, and relational space in which CLE participants can begin to come together and share their collective gifts in order to understand their collective challenges from multiple perspectives, and then to co-construct solutions to those challenges that, when enacted together, can lead to sustained and empowering action and change.

The Work of the Community Learning Exchange

Launched in 2008, this sustained work encourages communities to work across boundaries to cultivate collective leadership and local solutions to issues. Much of this work focuses on engaging the community to improve education as a vital pathway of opportunity and well-being for historically marginalized communities. A key component of this work is the inclusion of local communities sharing their approaches broadly with other organizations and communities. CLEs take place as national gatherings, as well as regional and local learning exchanges.

An early CLE brought 10 communities from states ranging from New York to Hawaii together in south Texas for a 3-day CLE focused on the theme "Collective Leadership and Systems Change: Examining Poverty, Practice, and Policy." About

70 people from different walks of life participated, including high school students, teachers, and principals; nonprofit workers; university professors; and parents concerned about their children's education. Two local community-based organizations, the Llano Grande Center for Research and Development and La Union del Pueblo Entero (LUPE), hosted the gathering. Together with the national CLE planning team, the host organizations planned the agenda, organized policy field trips as site visits, and designed a process for engagement that utilized interactive and place-based pedagogies. Local organizers understood the issues best and provided the local stories on how families, communities, and other sectors dealt with poverty; local participants were also interested in learning how other communities addressed similar issues. How and where the communities came together were key questions that informed how the agenda would be shaped and the physical locations where communities would engage in conversations. The issues mattered, the conversations mattered, and the spaces where ideas and conversations were shared mattered, as physical and metaphorical spaces were fundamental considerations to maximize the learning process.

Community in the Community Learning Exchange

In the CLE vernacular, community is a process as much as it is a physical, tangible place. Community is not something that stands alone but is a generative structure informed by a set of ideas, practices, struggles, hopes, and dreams. It is a set of questions that challenges assumptions, principles, and ways of being. Community is where we make meaning, transform meaning, and work together for the common good. It is where people come together with the intent to build, teach, and learn with each other. Community is a state of mind, a metaphorical expression of how people can be together. Pedagogies that are community-centered value people and tend to identify and build the agency they bring with them. One youth from South Texas described community by suggesting, "It's like *primos* (cousins) you never met before." The youth suggested we come from the same ancestors, some with different shades of skin color, some with different accents and languages. "But we're all the same," he said, "because we all hurt, we all laugh, and we can all celebrate what we are together." In the end, he suggested his greatest realization through the CLE experience is that community is about a way of life. It's about living a life where we invest in our relationships, recognize our gifts, explore our stories, respect our place, and do all this in an ethical manner. This is the meaning of "community" in the Community Learning Exchange.

The community of the CLE emerged from a Kellogg Foundation national leadership initiative called the Kellogg Leadership for Community Change (KLCC). Started in 2002 with the goal of building community leadership in some of the most distressed regions of the country, KLCC intended to use the Foundation's lessons on building local leadership capacities through a model of collective leadership for community change. The Foundation selected 11 communities for the initiative that spanned between 2002 and 2006. It identified two national organizations, the Center for Ethical Leadership (CEL) from Seattle and the Institute for Educational Leadership (IEL) from Washington, DC, to coordinate the national work. The national organizations played key roles in facilitating the leadership development through organizing national conferences, facilitating skill-building workshops, and holding the national community together. Both CEL and IEL played critical roles in supporting the Community Learning Exchange.

The expansion of the CLE network has been organic and generative. As the KLCC grant period came to an end, the communities banded together in a new collective iteration known as the Community Learning Exchange. The CLE family expanded from 11 communities to dozens of communities from at least a dozen states. The growth has typically occurred through a generative process where an original community invites a new community to participate in a CLE. Identifying new communities to participate depends on the relationship between the organizing theme for a particular CLE and the nature of leadership for community change in which a prospective community may be engaged. Readiness and vision are key dispositions for invitation. A community must have awareness that it wants to change and there must be a semblance of hope for change. The original communities looked for such qualities as they invited new communities into the process. For example, the original community from South Texas, named the Llano Grande Center, invited another community from Hawaii to participate in the South Texas CLE, because the Hawaiian community was involved in systems change initiatives through a close look at policy and poverty. A new community from California was invited to the South Texas CLE for the same reason, as were communities from the Bronx, New York, rural North Carolina, and Jacksonville, Florida. Each of the new communities demonstrated readiness to act and a vision to engage in leadership for the public good.

A close look at Jacksonville provides useful lessons in understanding the spirit and scope of learning exchanges. When a Jacksonville team designed their CLE, they built on several years of planning, organizing, and hosting of local learning exchanges. Through a multi-year process, local students, teachers, workers in the faith community, and others nurtured local interest in this interactive process for teaching and learning. Local CLEs were held in churches, community centers, and local universities, including a public university and a Historically Black College or University (HBCU). A series of community conversations locally identified the salient issues within the local economy and in the community at large, namely the chronic issue of racial strife and opportunities for African American youth in schools. Through deep discussions on the history of race relations in the region and the role of faith-based organizations, local leaders raised local awareness and began to reach out to others across the country to learn how other communities worked to resolve issues of race. Jacksonville leaders generated momentum and sought to host a national learning exchange focused on the theme of moral courage. Through their developmental experience, they realized that social and racial justice work required that participants exercise moral courage. They were ready to talk with both local folks, and with communities from across the country about how to share stories specific to moral courage, and how to move toward a future of hope and opportunity.

The Jacksonville team worked strategically with the national planning team to identify communities from different parts of the country and from northern Florida to participate in the Jacksonville learning exchange. "We're looking for communities that see themselves as morally courageous. We want them to be talking to each other, to learn from each other," said a Jacksonville teacher while on a conference call intended to recruit fitting communities. When the communities were identified, each was asked to bring a team from their place; typically, guest communities arrive in teams of four to six. In Jacksonville, like other CLEs, youth were highlighted as team members. In the end, the planning process called for 70 participants recruited from a dozen organizations or communities. Half would be locals, primarily from the Jacksonville area; the other half would come from the continental United States and from Hawaii. Identification of local themes was guided by the question, "Where have we seen moral courage exercised in authentic ways?" Jacksonville organizers subsequently probed the local networks and scanned the regional landscape. The same question guided identification of locations to engage in site visits, an important practice in the evolving CLE pedagogies.

Local organizations came from the state university, the local HBCU, faith-based organizations, social services agencies, and a community development enterprise. All local organizations had been engaged in conversations on issues of race, community, history, and how acts of moral courage have shaped those issues, so they were primed to share and learn. Others traveled long distances. They came from an organization in Seattle that facilitates social, cultural, and historical healing processes and other engagement practices. They came from a school in Central Texas where teachers and school leaders explore the historical roots of inequity in the school and community, and use the findings to shape school curriculum and pedagogies that are culturally relevant and responsible. They came from an organization in Washington, DC, where issues of special needs children across the country are addressed through policy advocacy. They came from Hawaii, where a team works to reverse the colonization forces of Native Hawaiian people through wide-ranging school reform initiatives that place Native Hawaiian culture at the center of teaching and learning. They came from South Texas, where a team of students and faculty members from a regional university work to integrate Mexican American historical and cultural themes into ways of teaching and learning at a school populated by 90% Mexican American students, but with minimal curricular presence of Mexican American themes across the university. All participating communities saw themselves as exercising moral courage as they pursued their social change agendas. Maintaining alignment to the theme, moral courage in the case of the Jacksonville CLE, is an important part of the planning process.

The work of the CLE has engendered a new brand of civic behavior based on trusting relationships, building assets, and creating new stories by focusing on place and inspiring community action. The work has unleashed a new imagination. A youth who attended the CLE in Jacksonville reflected on her newfound imagination when she said,

> I'd always thought the answers to fixing our problems needed to come from ideas outside our community. But after this experience, including the weeks before the three days of intense CLE work and the weeks after the actual gathering, I'm beginning to think all the answers are here. We just need to tap our imagination more than we have in the past. I've found that my imagination is most active and more creative when I think about all the good people and all the great talent we have in our own community. We have the answers to our problems.

Community Learning Exchanges are about uniting the power of place with the wisdom of people. This can only be done by bringing people together in conversation. During the CLE's early life, teachers, students, and parents from rural South Texas have come together with educators and parents from the Bronx, New York, to learn about how to build on existing local strengths; teachers and students from the island of Oahu have similarly come together with school leaders and students from Central Texas communities to fortify the institution building and community development work they do at home. Leaders from Jacksonville, Florida, rural northeast North Carolina, Seattle, Buffalo, Laguna Pueblo in New Mexico, Washington, DC, rural northwestern Wisconsin, and so many other places have come together to learn from each and to break the isolation of their day-do-day work; they've come together to find new solutions that are respectful, that understand the importance of place, that identify and build on local assets, and that weave stronger communities. People from these far-reaching places have built the skills and learned strategies and processes to do such things through their experience in the CLE.

Rhythm of CLE

The origins of the ideas fueling the CLE's imagination are articulated in its genealogy; the CLE works to unite the power of place with the wisdom of people.

When the elements outlined in this text merge, the spirit of the CLE comes alive. In this context, "coming to life" means that deep conversations take place, thoughtful questions guide the inquiry, relationships are developed, our imagination is enlarged, and the curriculum for engagement is dynamic. This section ties the different elements in the book into a logic model based on the rhythm of the CLE, as it deviates from the traditional step-by-step linear "how-to" model. The rhythm between place, people, and topic/theme is aligned by the CLE's curricular strategies applied by the planning and facilitation team.

In the stories of change and engagement outlined in this book, we see the CLE work in multiple spaces and for varying purposes. The stories can be couched within the ecologies of knowing that are individual, organization, and community, and they highlight varied pedagogical strategies employed in response to each situation and space. This transference of learning in action is the utility and wide-ranging practice of a CLE, but a CLE does not just happen. Each CLE story is shaped by an engagement process set to a rhythm prompted and inspired by a response to the local community, often to a community need, asset, condition, or opportunity. This is a critical step in making the work relevant, responsive, and sustainable.

Genealogy of the Community Learning Exchange

The CLE was a convergence of multiple sources. It started as the Kellogg Leadership for Community Change. By design, the Community Learning Exchange cultivates context and teaching and learning pedagogies that are time-tested and culturally relevant. Specifically, CLE pedagogies were developed from robust instructional approaches that are intergenerational, where elders and youth unite to explore how lessons from the past can help solve problems of the present.

The Community Learning Exchange also grew from the lessons of Myles Horton and the Highlander Folk School (later the Highlander Center for Research and Development), whose work serves as a guidepost. Like Highlander, CLEs embrace the need for strategies that honor the local wisdom of community members. Honoring the words and wisdom of Horton by putting them into practice, the Community Learning Exchange does not frame community work as missionary work. On the contrary, the Community Learning Exchange strives to develop and use strategies that empower local people in their own spaces to find solutions that are organic in order to meet the needs of the people that will live in and sustain healthy communities.

CLE pedagogies are also significantly informed by the wisdom of indigenous and other cultural models of collective leadership that similarly position family and close trusting networks at the center of personal, organizational, and community development approaches. In this respect, the long-term genesis of the

Community Learning Exchange has been shaped by the deep cultural and familial stories of those who led in its innovation. To recognize those stories and their impact on the shape and direction of the Community Learning Exchange, the next section uses personal and organizational stories from the Texas–Mexican border as experienced by authors Francisco and Miguel Guajardo to bring to life how they have shaped the development of the CLE. The personal stories come from their childhood in the late 1960s and early 1970s, when they came to this country as Mexican immigrants. The organizational stories come from the narrative of the Llano Grande Center for Research and Development. Together, these stories document and describe long-term incubation of visions and dreams that would be the soil in which the seeds of the CLE would later grow. Within this fertile soil of their childhood—the ideas learned by listening to the stories of their parents, the summers partially spent self-organizing their own baseball leagues while growing up in rural South Texas, and the dreams of a better story for their family and their community—the roots of the five axioms of the CLE and its theory of change began to take hold.

Guajardo Brothers History: Fertile Soil of the Community Learning Exchange

When they were in elementary school, a few years after having emigrated from Mexico, the Guajardo family (mother Julia, father José Angel, and four sons) became part of the migrant labor stream. One year they migrated to Buttonwillow, California, where the family worked hoeing weeds most of the summer; another summer they traveled to the Texas Panhandle, where they picked onions; and other summers they simply worked the fields in and around their hometown of Elsa in the Rio Grande Valley of South Texas. But the most formative summer was the one they spent in the labor camp in Keeler, a rural community in Southwestern Michigan. In Keeler their collective leadership skills began to grow.

Two interesting stories emerged from their time in Keeler, particularly from a child development and leadership formation perspective. Because they left South Texas sometime in early April, almost two months before the school year closed, they were obligated to enroll in a local school in Michigan. And they did, in a school in Sister Lakes, a charming coastal town by Lake Michigan. One story emerges from that schooling experience. The other comes from evening social activity at the labor camp.

Frequently in the evenings, the four Guajardo boys sat around in a circle outside the cabin at the labor camp, often with other children who lived in neighboring cabins, and told stories. The adults, including their parents, typically refereed the activity, ensured things were in order, and nurtured conditions so the kids could engage in a kind of safe, creative social activity. On many nights, they listened to radio broadcasts of Cincinnati Reds baseball games. The Reds were the

PHOTO 1.1 Guajardo Family circa 1972.

Source: Guajardo Family. Used with permission.

biggest show in professional sports during those days, the mid- to late 1970s, when Pete Rose, Joe Morgan, Johnny Bench, and others formed the core of the "Big Red Machine," the most feared baseball club of the era. Although Southwestern Michigan was a state away, the Guajardo transistor radio had a far reach and so the Reds' games extended across the airwaves on most clear summer nights, and the games provided prime material for great theater at the labor camp.

Their older brother Juan Jose, or "Pepe," as they call him, typically played the lead role as he mimicked Marty Brenneman, the Reds' play-by-play announcer. One of the younger kids usually performed the color commentating, à la Joe Nuxhall, Brenneman's on-air sidekick. Pepe was the skilled, play-by-play man of the family; he had honed his skills between the ages of five and seven as he listened to the Broncos de Reynosa baseball games on Mexican radio when the family lived south of the border. Pepe was quite the performer, using voice inflection, building drama, and providing thick descriptions of players and their nuances; some of it he learned from the radio announcers, some he simply made up.

The learning was rich. It was about baseball, but also about other subjects. They learned about math, like how to calculate batting averages, earned run averages, and more. If Pete Rose belted one hit in three times at bat, they knew he batted .333 that night. They also learned geography. When manager Sparky Anderson pulled his starting pitcher in the seventh inning and brought in relief pitcher Pedro Borbón from the bullpen, Brenneman was sure to note that Borbón hailed from the Dominican Republic, so the boys learned about the Dominican Republic. They learned where Oakland was on the map, because Joe Morgan came from there, and so on. Just as importantly, they learned about language, mainly the use of the English language, as they listened to Brenneman and Nuxhall. They learned pronunciation, syntax, and rhetorical devices, as baseball broadcasts are rich with creative wordsmithing.

Almost nightly at the labor camp, they learned how to perform. If a game played on the radio that night, Pepe would lead the performance by repeating much of what the announcers said. He would create during commercial breaks, while the other children imagined and provided color commentary to his Pepe's play-by-play narration. If the Reds had a night off, then it became pure original theater, as Pepe and his announcing crew created new baseball situations; the action in the room was detailed and intense. On those nights, the Reds never lost. And neither did the children at the camp.

The Guajardo parents and other adults from the labor camp were the producers of this theater. They ensured things were safe as the kids played the games and collectively created and imagined new plays and new games. The parents nurtured the conditions where the children could learn the skills and practice specific leadership functions, and where they could do it together. This became their rich training ground for collective leadership.

During the day, they went to school in Sister Lakes. A yellow school bus stopped outside the camp every morning to pick them up, the migrant kids. Just about every one of the migrant kids was Mexican or Mexican American, with the possible exception of two kids, who may have been poor Whites. The bus took them to the school in Sister Lakes, where the migrant kids got off the bus and walked to a side door of the schoolhouse that led them to the migrant classroom in the basement. All the migrant kids went to the basement. They typically stayed in that room the entire day, except for lunchtime—the only time when migrant students saw the first floor of the school. The migrant classroom included all grade levels. First graders joined second, third, and even eighth graders in that basement classroom. Altogether, more than 40 migrant students filled the crowded basement classroom led by a teacher and a teacher aide.

The teachers were very nice. They seemed to care, showing kindness and sensitivity to the students. The classroom rules were fairly standard. The teaching and learning process typically followed the teaching practices that Martin Haberman has come to call "a pedagogy of poverty," where students sit in rows, listen passively to the teacher, and are asked to memorize facts and then regurgitate them on a test. That was the mode of operation in the migrant classroom.

Most importantly, they were in the basement. That's the lingering memory—that the migrant kids went to school in the basement. They typically did not mix with the other students, the locals who were not part of the migrant experience. Their classrooms were on the first and second floors and in the light. The migrant students rarely saw them, except for glimpses as they came into the schoolhouse in the morning and as they left in the afternoon. It was clear enough to the migrant students that they were treated differently, perhaps even in a manner consistent with segregationist practices. It is difficult to measure the impact of this reality, though we know the preponderance of evidence suggests that segregationist practices in schools have deep psychological effects on children. The legal and social discourse that surrounded the historic 1954 *Brown v. Board of Education* Supreme Court case elevated into the public consciousness the argument that segregation and its practices adversely affect the psychology of children. Sending migrant students to the basement constituted a practice of segregation in this particular school, an experience tantamount to the experience other children in parts of the Jim Crow South experienced in schools and even in social life. The migrant student life in Southwestern Michigan was very similar. In the mid-1970s, this schooling experience exposed migrant students, and the Guajardos specifically, to the underbelly of their enlightened society. They would have been in serious trouble if this had been the extent of their educational life as well as the source of their assets, strengths, and gifts.

Fortunately, this was not the extent of their daily educational experience, because after school the bus took them back to the labor camp where they prepared for a richer, deeper learning process around storytelling. The Cincinnati Reds games on the radio offered one excuse around which to convene "class." But on the "off" nights when the Reds were not on the radio, that was when Pepe and the labor camp kids were most "on." On those nights, Pepe created his own play-by-play, others provided color commentary, and they generally told stories. In those creative scenarios that their parents and other adults nurtured, the conditions were clear: egalitarian impulses were encouraged, participation was expected, and they exercised leadership in a collective way. This was the other emergent story, the one filled with light and juxtaposed with the basement experience.

Back home in South Texas, the Guajardos lived in the federal housing projects, where they enjoyed a rich experience. They grew up and learned with other kids about leadership, teamwork, organization, and fun through the act of play. They organized their summer baseball league, fall football activities, winter basketball games, and *trompos* (tops) and *canicas* (marbles) tournaments held throughout the year. The youth who participated in these activities organized, implemented, and took care of the play. They talked about which kids would play on which teams; they secured hoes, shovels, hammers, and nails from their parents to level off the baseball infield; they mounted an old bicycle rim to a basketball backboard; and they trimmed a grass line for the goal-line gridiron. They created schedules and gathered enough money to buy balls, bats, or gloves they might need for the season. They self-organized their own play and their team sports activities. In so doing, they owned every part of the process and enjoyed it in the deepest way possible. These formative stories kindled their interest in community leadership.

When they left home to go to college in the early 1980s, Miguel and Francisco took their friends from their hometowns of Elsa and Edcouch and found friends from other parts of the world. While in college, they began to shape the story that one day they would come back home to take part in rebuilding their community. The dream became clearer after college, when they returned. They came back with a renewed sense of self and were a little more global in their thinking; they had grown up a bit more at the university in the big city, had studied abroad, and traveled to several continents of the world. By the early 1990s, their love for their hometown, devotion to the stories of their childhood, and lessons learned from their formal studies and travels all melded into a clearer vision. The vision gained greater clarity in classrooms at Edcouch-Elsa High School, when they began to enact some of their lifelong ideas—ideas about building their own stories as individuals and members of a community, and doing that with students through the use of specific curricular and pedagogical approaches.

They claim that coming back home was a gift, just as it was a challenge and an opportunity. Their upbringing had taught them the power of stories, the wisdom and compassion of the people, and the charm in the narrative of the town. In their context, that was the hidden opportunity. The challenge was that most townspeople did not see their story as a source of personal power or as an asset, nor did they view their community as a unique and special place. Students at the high school reflected this perspective, as they were mired in a notion that they could not dream big about going to college. The sense of low expectations was palpable and even seemed endemic. To be sure, much of this stemmed from the socio-economic condition and isolation of the community and region.

For more than a generation this region had earned the dubious distinction as the most economically impoverished area in the country, and the steady influx of immigration from south of the Texas–Mexican border continued (and continues) to populate the region with people of limited economic or other material means. From a regional perspective, the place had gained a clear identity as a result of a century-long agri-business economy that essentially defined a two-tiered economic and social structure comprising (a) a ruling class and (b) a working class. The Guajardos were raised in and were full participants in the two-tiered structure of working the agricultural fields and were shaped by that reality.

This two-tiered setting nurtured a dominant narrative in their community. It was a narrative of power, where the landowners and farmers wielded the power and manual workers followed the orders of the powerful. The power dynamic was also largely informed by race, as Anglos (Whites) constituted the vast majority of the ruling class, while the Mexicans and Mexican Americans populated the working class. Social structures and life similarly reflected the two-tiered system in ways that starkly resembled the social and political rules of the Jim Crow American South, where segregation reigned supreme. There was the school for White children and the "Mexican" school; there was the White theater and the Cine

Mexicano. This was as much the South as it was the American Southwest. The economic and social conditions supported the dominant narrative. In that narrative, Mexican and Mexican American children were not encouraged to think about going to college, much less an exclusive college—that notion was antithetical to the dominant narrative.

Slowly, however, that narrative began to crack. For the Guajardos this happened too slowly. Even as Mexican American students began to attend college, they typically did so as a gradual step; that is, they only thought about the possibility of going to technical school or to the local college. In this emerging story of college, there was little space to leap far beyond the base expectation. The psychological impact of the two-tiered society engrained, in the minds and souls of many local people, the idea that they could not reach high, that they could not dream big. This was an insidious social construction that had to be reversed. The Guajardo vision was governed by the stories they heard as children, stories generated through the same social and economic structures, but told and understood in radically different ways. It was told to them as a counter-story. This was the other side of the dominant narrative, the part they were exposed to in their upbringing.

The counter-story was the goods their parents and others elders shared with them. The elders told about how they worked tirelessly to clear the tough South Texas brush to build new towns. They told stories of how they worked the fields in order to feed their families, but also to feed an entire nation during wartime. They heard stories of hard working people who persevered in the face of adversity, raised healthy and well-adjusted families, and participated in most facets of social and civic life. The range of stories was impressive, as they were delivered through multiple *pláticas* told as jokes, songs, poems and, as their father called them, "*tragedias y comedias*" (tragedies and comedies). They were told around the dinner table, on the front porch, and sometimes at the local coffee shop. On occasion, they learned from stories transmitted through the radio, though they were often filtered through their parents. These were genuine stories of the human spirit. They were real "American" stories.

This part of the narrative was not typically talked about in schools, or in the popular media, nor were they reflected in the market culture. But this was the uplifting part of the broader narrative, the part that could inspire children and elders, and move communities that had been mired in social and economic degradation toward a new and more enlightened existence. The challenge was to rehabilitate the dominant narrative, and they saw the school as an appropriate laboratory through which to do so. They felt a responsibility to employ the lessons learned from their elders, from the rest of the community, and through their higher education experience. They would use the combination of these lessons to build a formal pedagogy that would also become a community development strategy.

Family History and Story to the Re-imagined Community Organization

Miguel and Francisco Guajardo felt the need to take a big leap if they were to change the community story in a bold way. The challenge was to use the stories of community knowledge, wisdom, and strengths to cultivate a new kind of expectation for students and, by extension, raise the collective level of expectation of the community. In this context, the Llano Grande Center was born. Llano Grande began as a college preparation program to prepare students so they could get into schools such as Harvard, Yale, Columbia, Stanford, and MIT. Through Llano Grande the Guajardos built a curriculum grounded in the exploration of story, identity formation, and community-based research, and used this as the curricular framework through which students learned the three Rs. They believed that students from this South Texas community, many of whom came from immigrant and/or migrant families, possessed the talent and ability to do well in the best colleges in the country. They just had to believe they could.

More than two decades later, after placing dozens of students in Ivy League universities, and after raising the college-bound rate of graduating seniors from Edcouch-Elsa High School by more than 100%, the narrative shifted. In the new millennium local youth feel as if they have the permission to dream big about where to go to college and what they want to do with their lives. As importantly, many students now view their community as a place with value, and many imagine better days to come. The old two-tiered story has given way to a more egalitarian social and economic construct wherein more local residents, including youth, participate in the life of their community. The story of the two-tiered structure was driven by a few who made decisions about economy, education, and local policy. The new narrative is an emerging model where collective action and leadership are much more respected as modalities through which community change is exacted.

The story of the Llano Grande is the story of building power, a narrative that departs from a controlling and debilitating scheme that benefitted only a few to a system that values deeper participation by a greater number of people. The new narrative is built on the strengths and wisdom of local people, both young and old, and affirmatively positions those who have been historically marginalized at the center of constructing new meaning.

Llano Grande: A Story of Community Growth and Power

A few years ago I went to a Community Learning Exchange with a group of local parents. It was held in South Texas, and it was the experience that initiated a lot of the changes in our communities, changes that have now spread county-wide," said a CLE alumna who worked with a group of South Texas residents to change the political behavior of county government. He added, "We learned how to build our team so that would advocate for a bond issue to build new schools. We accomplished our goals to build new schools. Today, we're changing how we invest vast resources that impact well over a million people in this county."

The preceding vignette was born out of the experience of a rural community in South Texas in the midst of unprecedented growth and rapid social change. The story is also a product of the evolving work of the Llano Grande Center. The mission was to place students from this high school in college, even the best colleges in the country. Llano Grande quickly gained national renown as dozens of students, largely Mexican American youth, gained admission into Ivy League and other prestigious universities. By the mid-1990s the organization transformed its college preparation toward work focused on building academic and other critical skills for college through a place-based curriculum centered on the lives of students and the local community. In such a curricular approach, the process of teaching and learning revolved around helping students understand their personal, family, and community stories. Social studies and language arts classes looked at building critical thinking, writing, and other communication skills through careful study of people, events, and significant entities located in the community. Science and math classes similarly investigated local flora, fauna, and climate; looked at the width and height of physical structures; and closely observed other local assets as a way to learn how to compute, read and write, understand climate, and appreciate science. More importantly, the curiosity and imagination of children and educators alike were nurtured through a methodology that valued the people and community of children and adults involved in the teaching and learning (see *Video Links* for video about the Llano Grande Center).

Within a few years after its founding, Llano Grande acquired a property with renowned education anthropologist Enrique Trueba. After retiring as a distinguished professor at the University of Texas at Austin, Trueba moved to South Texas to immerse himself in the work of Llano Grande. Since the late 1990s, the Llano Grande property has served as a training ground for local educators, community activists, and nonprofit leaders from across the country.

Llano Grande operates on the understanding that when students learn their own reality through a process of critical self-reflection, they can use that realization as a source of strength and as an advantage to gain access to higher education. Students learned through exercises in writing and storytelling, listening to stories of others, and collecting oral histories from community elders. Understanding oneself emerged as a centerpiece of the Llano Grande theory of change, a theory embraced and used by the CLE that incubates the "self" in the middle of the "ecologies of knowing." The "organization" and the "community" comprise two other "ecologies of knowing," and form the other cornerstones of the place-based curriculum. Through this course of youth development, students understand how

PHOTO 1.2 Painting of Llano Grande House by Brenda Engel.

Source: Brenda Engel. Used with permission.

to build their story. They learn how to nurture relationships and work to build personal and other local assets, helping them gain value and appreciation for the place in which they live—their community. This place-based approach to college preparation gained significant success and traction locally as national foundations saw this work in South Texas as a model to share across the country, and possibly replicate in willing communities.

Llano Grande parlayed the success of its college preparation program into its emerging leadership and community development initiatives. As it began to work with schools and communities across the region and eventually in other parts of the country, the organization stayed close to it philosophical roots—understand yourself first, then work to understand the organization and the community. The early work on community leadership development with other local partners posed challenges, primarily because participants involved in leadership development typically wanted to leap into project planning and implementation. The way of the Llano Grande called for more formative work focused on building the self, building relationships, and building trust with others. Just as going inward proved to be an effective strategy toward college preparation with high school students, the organization believed it imperative that community leadership participants pursue a similar approach.

When Llano Grande entered its first community leadership program, it ensured conditions were ripe for healthy community building. As it worked with 25 participants in its leadership program, the organization scheduled several months of community building exercises through which participants were strategically led to share their life stories with each other. The result was the formation of trusting relationships between leadership program participants. Exercises in understanding local history and culture were similarly practiced so that participants gained clarity about local context and ecology. When leadership participants embarked upon the study and review of local issues, the conditions for community change work had been established. People knew and trusted each other, and they had a working understanding of context. Participants were engaged in a community of practice, because they participated in building leadership for community change.

Summary

Regardless of their specific use at any given time, the narratives in this book also represent a simple affirmation: our stories and our histories matter. Stories matter because they serve as our primary way of making sense of our world. Stories matter because they help us build and sustain relationships. Stories matter because they inform us about place. And stories matter because they help us see possibilities and hope beneath layers of despair. They help us find courage when we are frightened. And stories help us find agency when we feel powerless.

These genealogical narratives of the Community Learning Exchange and the experiences and histories that have given birth to it serve many functions. The accounts of the Guajardo family history, the Llano Grande Center, community practices of indigenous cultures, and the work of Myles Horton and the Highlander Folk School all serve as rich sources for the CLE theory of change, and the ecologies of knowing. At the same time, these same stories can be used to illustrate axiomatic aspects of the CLE work because they most certainly have informed them. Inversely, we believe that these stories should also be used as a context through which a deeper meaning of the Community Learning Exchange can be made.

References and Further Readings

Block, P. (2009). *Community: The structure of belonging.* San Francisco, CA: Berrett-Koehler.

Guajardo, M., & Guajardo, F. (2002). Critical ethnography and community change. In Y. Zou & H. Trueba (Eds.), *Ethnography and schools: Qualitative approaches to the study of education* (pp. 281–304). Lanham, MD: Rowman & Littlefield.

Guajardo, M., & Guajardo, F. (2008). Two brothers in higher education: Weaving a social fabric for service in academic—A model of interdependence. In R. Padilla & K. Gonzalez (Eds.), *Latino perspectives on higher education for the public good: An intergenerational approach* (pp. 60–81). Herndon, VA: Stylus.

Guajardo, F., & Guajardo, M. (2010). Cultivating stories of change. In K. Ruder (Ed.), *Weaving strong communities: The collective leadership storybook* (pp. 85–103). Seattle, WA: Center for Ethical Leadership.

Guajardo, F., & Guajardo, M. (2013). The power of Platica. *Reflections: A Journal of Public Rhetoric, Civic Writing, and Service Learning, 13*(1), 159–164.

Haberman, M. (1991). The pedagogy of poverty versus good teaching. *Phi Delta Kappan, 73*(4), 290–294.

Habermas, J. (1984). *The theory of communicative action* (Vol. 2, T. McCarthy, Trans.). Boston, MA: Beacon Press.

Horton, M., Freire, P., Bell, B., Gaventa, J., & Peters, J. (1990). *We make the road by walking: Conversations on education and social change.* Philadelphia, PA: Temple University Press.

Jacobs, D. (2003). *The Myles Horton reader: Education for social change.* Knoxville: University of Tennessee Press.

2

MEANING MAKING, AXIOMS, AND ECOLOGIES FOR ENGAGEMENT

We come to this work acknowledging the power of place and the wisdom of people; we are educators, activist academics, and parents. We bring our experiences and remember the spirit of our childhood. This spirit includes the view that play is children's work and is at the heart of how we engage, activate, and build relationships that then nourish our individual and collective development. Fun is at the core of engagement and engagement is a core value of the CLE work highlighted in this text. We have lived the reality that when people are invited to share their stories as they author themselves, their wisdom radiates with excitement in a public way. Certainly the intensity and complexity of our realities vary, but the building elements of learning and teaching in public remain the same. This public and collective learning yields a power that is inviting and contagious.

Importance of Meaning Making

At the CLE, we are deliberate about how we inform and navigate the learning and meaning-making process. Emerging from our understanding that relationships are central to our work through the CLE, we begin from the shared belief and conception that the learning process is first and foremost social. We manage this stage by inviting teams to participate in a CLE. We deviate from the individual framing of this learning experience because we are deliberate about maximizing the social aspect of the learning experiences. When attending an event as a team, we also maximize the opportunity for conversation, reflection, and exploration. This is a benefit of the collective leadership process. Vygotsky tells us that we experience an event twice, first socially and then cognitively. As we scaffold the meaning-making process at the CLE, we add to this experience by expanding the social aspects of learning by designing and engaging in a dynamic, generative learning experience. It is through the relationships being developed that the cognitive experience of co-constructing knowledge occurs. This social and cognitive learning process is informed by opportunities to story the experiences, reflect upon the experience, re-author or re-narrate the experience and, finally, act on the experience. Within this final, crucial component of the learning experience the technical aspects concerning *how* we act upon ourselves, our families, our organizations, our institutions, and our communities begin to take form. This, too, is a deeply collaborative process in which the approaches, strategies, and solutions that arise from the individual, idiosyncratic imaginations and contexts of the participants are shared, in order to form a composite set of robust options and opportunities that these individual teams can then take back with them and enact within themselves, their organizations, and their communities.

When convening a CLE, participants bring their stories, experiences, questions, and passions to the gathering. The CLE uses the organic elements of our guiding axioms and transfers them to a place of hosting. Through the collective process of bringing these axioms to life, the CLE becomes a process for convening diverse groups of people and ideas across traditional and artificial boundaries including places, cultures, ages, and realities. The meaning-making process of a CLE begins well before teams of participants show up to the CLE. The planning process is collaborative, generative, and dialogical. The process, from beginning to end and beyond (i.e., debriefing of the engagement experience and implementation of action plans), is deliberate and designed to continuously nurture conversations intended to help participants explore, change, and grow. This engagement process—or pedagogy, if you will—is effective when we help develop a schema for participants to organize conversations conceptually, name experiences, make meaning of these experiences, and act upon them. We use the axioms of the CLE below to nurture this process and inform the learning. We acknowledge the CLE process described earlier departs from the traditional educational experiences many of us have lived in public institutions. However, it is this critically important departure that allows for the organic experiences of the CLE to be brought to life.

Axioms That Guide the Work

At the core of the work are five axioms. We believe these concepts to be truths that form the core of the CLE value system. We use these *axioms* here in purposeful ways. The axioms frame the beginning of the work, and they also become evident through experiencing a CLE. Borrowing its meaning within its uses in modern logic, an axiom can be thought of *as a beginning* or starting point. The work of the CLE begins with these guiding values, though the use of the axioms also transcends the calculating constraints of modern logic that would limit them as simply the beginning of the work of the CLE.

We reach for a deeper meaning of axioms used by philosophers in ancient Greece. For them and for us, an axiom is a truth without any need for proof in the form of linear logic. For us, these *axioms are established by means of real, lived experiences.* When friends, family, and other community members want to learn about the CLE, we can describe the process and we can share these axioms, but it is only through experiencing a CLE that these axioms first become true and real.

The core values represented by these axioms permeate boundaries while guiding thought, practice, and relationships. They are always at work in a circular, non-linear way. The CLE work is neither a project nor an isolated event—*it is a way of life.* The rest of this chapter is the scaffolding to the meaning-making process we employ at the CLE. We seek here to help the reader make the best sense of this social innovation and the life that emerges when at work within a CLE, in absence of having yet truly experienced it.

In our attempt to approximate the experience of the CLE, we use stories in this book to reveal how these axioms can be a guiding force, a way of life. While living

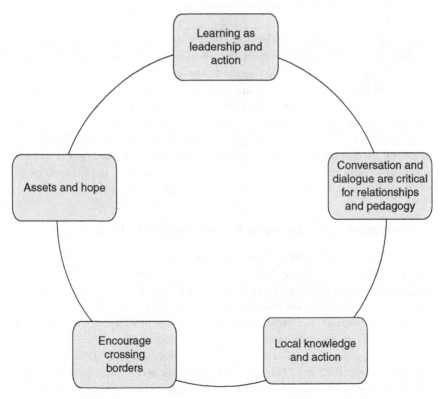

FIGURE 2.1 CLE axioms

by these axioms does not always guarantee success, it does provide an opportunity to expand our understanding of the world in a dignified way. A working understanding and acceptance of this way of living yields an opportunity to notice events, conversations, and invitations we have not noticed before developing this awareness. A working understanding and acceptance of this way of living also yields the consciousness and spirit needed to design and nurture the work of the CLE for others to experience first so that they can live it too.

Learning and Leadership Are a Dynamic Social Process

Organizers of the CLE believe learning is a leadership act and that leadership is at its best when it is in collaborative action. This duality informs the dynamic nature of the pedagogical process. All participants have something to contribute, and they are active in framing their learning. This includes the stories they exchange; the conversations they share; the questions they frame; and the action plans they construct for themselves, their organizations, and their community. We see shared learning as the foundational action for the development and sustainability of human beings and the improvement of their social, economic, and political condition.

Learning how to learn within the context of relationships is at the core of leadership and the construction of the necessary conditions that nurture this development in an inviting and dignified manner. Learning emerging from, and within, relationships is supported and nurtured through a number of signature CLE pedagogies and is limited only by the distinct needs of the collective and the imaginations of the designers. Among the pedagogies, we have found that play provides distinct and powerful opportunities to support the development of relationships that transcend gender, culture, and generations. Not only does play allow us to connect to our universal "child" and the wonder and enthusiasm of seeing things with fresh eyes but it does so in democratizing ways.

Conversations Are Critical and Central Pedagogical Processes

At the core of social learning theory is the need to create safe spaces and healthy relationships for participants, learners, and teachers alike to share their stories. Relationships are the first point of contact in the learning process, and storytelling and conversation are the mediating tools. If the climate, spirit, and interaction between participants, facilitator, and/or their environment are not inviting and safe, it is difficult for sustainable and public learning to take place. This space is critically important for honest conversation and storytelling. It allows CLE participants to trust their story has value and will be respected. This safe space allows for critical points of view to be presented; this relational space invites the storytelling process and authentic, challenging conversation to take place.

The building blocks of CLE pedagogy include safe environment, storytelling, conversations, and relationships. This foundation of engagement helps participants develop and move to finding or building their voice toward action. Our challenge is to help co-create space to explore, imagine, and create alternative realities within the familiar. It is through our relationships with others that we change, grow, and develop. CLE pedagogies are designed to maximize opportunity and encouragement in order to build new relationships and nurture existing ones. Along with storytelling and conversations, there is an art to how we frame questions before, during, and after the CLE. Questions are used to encourage participants to see hidden personal strengths, to understand new possibilities, and to discover previously buried assets. Taken in full, conversations using questions and stories purposefully to support participant development and greater understanding of their situations within their home communities can yield healthy change.

The People Closest to the Issues Are Best Situated to Discover Answers to Local Concerns

As the CLE organizes around a certain topic, participants are invited and expected to engage with each other through sharing their individual and community stories and experiences around the CLE topic. Such engagement fosters a creative agency that helps people find their power and voice, and the process responds to the need for local communities to own their destiny, though not in an individualistic manner. On the contrary, theirs is a collective destiny. This collective process puts the power back into the hands of the people most impacted by the conditions and decision of the day. Here, the learning processes and experiences are developed in order to frame questions, conversations, and other pedagogical activities in age-appropriate, context-responsive, and culturally sustainable ways.

The CLE organizers believe people residing in local communities know the issues first hand and therefore need to be fully involved in constructing the organizing focus and selecting the pedagogies to these issues. We do not intend to oversimplify this process and suggest that, if they simply show up, CLE participants will magically find the answers. However, we do know that when people share their stories in public with those who have similar experiences from different communities, from different generations, or with different gifts, a collective and creative energy and focus take shape.

This collective and creative deviance takes place in a variety of crucial ways. First and foremost, the CLE provides opportunities for participants and their teams to return to their local communities prepared to deviate from the approaches, strategies, and actions that have not yielded the results and development. In doing so, these returning CLE participants infuse new ideas and possibilities into their home communities. This interjection of new hopes, approaches, strategies, and actions are innovations within these communities that can then spread contagiously to other community members, organizations, and institutions. Notably, the process by which participants and their teams have arrived at these new approaches, strategies, and actions is usually a deviation from how they have been developed in the past. Rather than isolated initiatives *acting on* community and largely informed by those learning, working, and living within it, the process of community change is now conceptualized as a collective endeavor in which the former CLE participants work to ensure that they are *acting with* their communities and the diverse perspectives and gifts within them. In sum, the CLE holds the potential to transform the *how* of community change, thus shifting the traditional, consolidated power dynamic to a collective action.

Crossing Boundaries Enriches the Development and Educational Process

The ability and willingness to experience a world that is outside our daily comfort zone is necessary to break the isolation of people, teams, and organizations. This dynamic is familiar and easier to comprehend when we invite teams to join national CLEs, but it becomes more difficult to articulate when we host local CLEs. The traditional border crossing we reference includes but is not limited to geographic borders; economic borders; age, culture, and racial borders; gender; faith; and differing abilities.

This border-crossing concept becomes more difficult to notice and articulate when everyone in the room looks like each other and lives in the same community, including the facilitators. Within this context, the facilitators' ability to make the familiar strange is important. This process happens when the meeting place and space is altered; the teaching is shifted from traditional lecture mode to one that is dialogical, experiential, collaborative, and engaged. This border crossing of ideas, questions, and learning processes is critically important to decenter the status quo and the traditional ways of knowing. This shift begins to rupture the comfort, status quo, and equilibrium we reach when a generative and dynamic conversation is missing from our institutional lives. This shift is also a move toward expanding our curiosity and imagination.

This process begins to invite and excite the curiosity of the learners. When community members are presented with a different language, mannerisms, and questions, they begin to accept the challenge to engage in the behavior themselves and construct their own questions. Even if they are not versed to frame specific questions, the invitation to express and exercise essential human curiosity is enough to begin. This is the magic of going to different places physically, emotionally, intellectually, and relationally. We witness this, too, with CLE participants.

Hope and Change Are Built on Assets and Dreams of Locals and their Communities

We have learned that when CLE participants tell their own story, they begin to map their gifts, ideas, hopes, and wishes. This mapping includes ideological, relational, and geographical skills, riches, wishes, and assets. The identification, naming, and construction of these assets invite CLE participants to view their work and their community in different ways. Issues that have historically been assumptions immediately become opportunities, invitations, and points of action. Transforming one's mind and consciousness from distress and hopelessness to hope and possibilities is, by definition, the most radical transformation we witness during the CLE experience. The exchange gives participants a new language, a different way of looking at the world, and a network of support that expands their community of practice while simultaneously breaking the isolation. In short, this reframing of our daily conditions from deficits to assets helps build hope and possibilities.

Moreover, this border-crossing within a semi-structured environment of a CLE becomes a space full of possibilities. Community members begin to develop a language that describes their experiences. They do so by using stories and imagination to both examine and reimagine their lived experiences and, thus, create alternate and multiple future possibilities.

Ecologies of Knowing

By the end of the CLE, participants experience a wide range of conversations, relationships, field site visits, questions, epiphanies, and moments of tension. These encounters test the multiple pieces of knowledge we rarely make public or export in traditional educational settings, including the cognitive, emotional, relational, critical, cultural, and historical. This intense engagement can push anyone into sensory overload, but we attempt to balance and navigate the learning within the following ecologies. We know that not all CLE participants will understand and/ or utilize this framework, because we are all at different levels of our own development. However, the CLE organizers work to balance the learning within three central ecologies of knowing: self, organizations, and communities.

These three ecologies organize our thinking and learning experiences from the micro to the meso and on to the macro levels, or spheres, in which we experience life. Like life itself, these ecologies are bordered by permeable boundaries that leave room for exchange and interplay, but serve their purpose when making meaning of the engagement before, during, and after the CLE. These ecologies are not isolated. They spiral inward and upward, weaving within a developmental process as our experiences inform our schema. The visual representation is a top view, but looking at this process from a side view, one can also see an image of a cone with a spiral-connecting strand from the bottom foundation to the tip

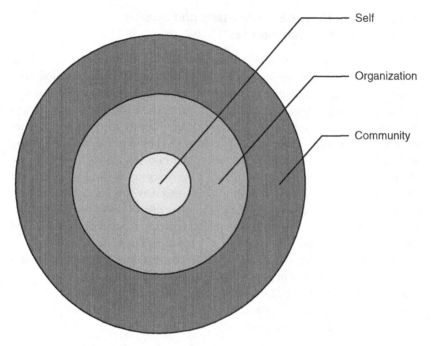

FIGURE 2.2 Ecologies of knowing

at the top of the cone, or the bottom, depending on your position of privilege or perspective. This spiral weaves the ecologies and our lived experiences into a cohesive yet developmental complexity that is both simple and dynamic in its construction.

Self

As learners, the self is the basis of the world of knowing. Within a collective leadership philosophy that we have framed and practiced, there is a constant balance, or tension, between the "I" and the "we." This is not presented as a binary but rather as a space that is both "I" and "we" at once, yet still a third space all the time. To negotiate this dynamic space, it is important that the individual have a solid foundation. This foundation includes the ability to filter information and make decisions in the best interest of the self and the organization. To accomplish this, the leaders must be in rhythm with their multiple ecologies.

We also believe that our individual constructions of self are invariably and essentially informed by our families. It is within our families that our sense of the collective first forms. We learn that others are necessary to meet our needs, and that it is through our relationships with others that we grow, change, and develop.

We also learn through family that we grow and develop through our relationships, not only from what we receive, but also from what we give. Family is the original learning exchange for us. It is the context for our learning about the self and also about the social world around us. As such, we see profound value in the native Hawaiian saying shared with us that to first understand our roles in society, we must first understand our roles in our family. To push that relationship even further, we have observed, learned, and experienced that our families shape who we are and both inform and are informed by the world—a dynamic that is shaped and sharpened by the CLE.

Organization

This meso frame is critical to honor our commitment to being a public people. We grow up in organizations and as educators know families, schools, churches, and other social collectives become mediating entities between the self and the larger society. These institutions and groups are critical to welcoming young people to the world, and the CLE plays this role for youth and adults alike. The CLE also serves as a mediating force for participants between many variables. It mediates between old understandings and new conceptions; passivity and engagement; obedience and empowerment; the status quo and a life of action; and, ultimately, oppression and liberation in a dynamic way.

Community

The world at the macro level impacts our daily lives in good and stressful ways. Knowing the flow of forces and locations of power in our lives and communities is important in informing our work and action plans and the hope that life can change. As we have written before, to know that there is dialogue between the micro and the macro in a reciprocal way is valuable in informing our future actions and questions. This is an empowering dialogue that communicates and makes known our abilities to bring about change in our communities and world if we act collectively with one another. This understanding shifts the relationship with community from an external and immutable constraint to a web of interwoven relationships that can be influenced to become more nurturing and just. It is within community that we live and grow, so the healthier our communities, the more effective and just nurturers they become.

Weaving and Scaffolding the Ecologies

The ability to negotiate the ecologies in a seamless way requires an understanding of relationships and knowing of each other's stories. In a CLE, we have learned that asking the right questions is more important than having the answers. When we

ask the right questions, CLE participants will find answers or a process informing where to go to uncover their need to learn and subsequently explore future
inquiry. The weaving of the ecologies becomes a developmental process where we
learn to make meaning of private and public experiences cognitively, emotionally,
and in a relational way with the world. This spiral process is simultaneously generative and summative in a human and community development manner.

Summary

The Community Learning Exchange, although first experienced as an event
occurring in an afternoon, day, or series of days, is much more than an isolated
project or event: *It is a way of life.* Specifically, it is a way of life that challenges our
thoughts, actions, practices, and relationships so that they might better support
the development of healthier selves, organizations, and communities. It is a way
of life that proposes *we learn best from real, lived experiences, and authentic and honest
relationships.*

Working from the fundamental and radical assumption that the people closest
to the issues are those best situated to address those issues and discover answers
to the concerns that arise from them, the CLE invites us to experience and live
through relationships that allow us to experience learning and leading as dynamic
social processes, and have conversations for pedagogical purposes. When people
participate in CLEs, they explore how they can cross boundaries in efforts to collectively construct solutions for organizational and community challenges that
unfetter and mobilize the assets, strengths, and dreams of community members.
These efforts toward collective solutions developed to generate constructive and
equitable changes in organizations and communities are supported by the five
axioms of the Community Learning Exchange and framed within our three
ecologies of knowing. These axiomatic principles become even more self-evident
when lived and experienced, and the ecologies of knowing allow for the CLE
participants to perceive and understand the various levels in which they are experiencing the problems they have, the challenges they face, and the way their lives
are impacted and shaped by those problems and challenges. However, although
the Community Learning Exchange begins with foundational axioms and ways
of understanding the ecologies of our lives and experiences, because the goals of
the CLE and those who form and attend them are to impact and change their
circumstances and institutions that shape them, something else is needed. For participants at a CLE to engage in change processes for their organizations and communities, an understanding, a theory, of change is essential. In the next chapter,
the Community Learning Exchange theory of change, developed from the efforts
and engagement of the Llano Grande Center for Research and Development, is
described and explored.

References and Further Readings

Argyris, C. (1992). *On organizational learning.* Cambridge, MA: Blackwell Business.

Kretzmann, J., & McKnight, J. (1993). *Building communities from the inside out: Path toward finding and mobilizing a community's assets.* Chicago, IL: ACTA.

March, J.G. (1999). Exploration and exploitation in organizational learning. In J.G. March (Ed.), *The pursuit of organizational intelligence* (pp. 114–136). Malden, MA: Blackwell.

Schon, D. (1983). *The reflective practitioner.* New York, NY: Basic Books.

Sergiovanni, T. (2000). *The lifeworld of leadership: Creating culture, community and personal meaning in our schools.* San Francisco, CA: Jossey-Bass.

Vygotsky, L. S. (1962). *Thought and language.* Cambridge, MA: MIT Press.

Weick, K. (1995). *Sensemaking in organizations.* Thousand Oaks, CA: Sage.

3

A THEORY OF CHANGE IN ACTION

The Community Learning Exchange (CLE) theory of change values relationships, assets, and places. Building community through such a theory of change and action anchors the work of the CLE and portends a community-building approach that moves away from community development based on deficit thinking models. Beyond the three ecologies, the CLE encourages schools and community-based organizations to look at issues of curriculum and pedagogies situated in the local context. Schools across the country that have become immersed in the work of the CLE have transformed themselves into places of innovation where teachers, students, and parents can work together to improve their hometowns. As a result, communities and schools have been better for it. Teaching and learning processes have focused on building community-based enterprises and on creating safe spaces where local residents can speak honestly on issues of race, class, gender, and other critical issues facing communities. Schools and non-profit organizations have partnered to build strong learning action teams and the public will to pass bond issues to build new schools, improve local and regional infrastructures, and address issues of wellness.

Community leadership and community change are complex propositions. People come and go, organizations come and go, and businesses change; the result is that communities, even the most remote, are in constant flux. The Community Learning Exchange theory of change attempts to understand the complexities of change as it looks at the formation of community leadership. Throughout the course of this book, the readers sees elements of the CLE theory of change and action. Early in the book, the critical nature and vitality of *relationships* are emphasized as essential to the life of the CLE. The spirit of the CLE experience is guided by the necessity to find what is good in people and communities. We call this *assets*-based development. *Stories* become the strategy and practice through which we identify assets, and stories tell us how those assets are developed. Community, or *place*, incubates the assets and stories, and becomes the nexus through which all these elements are enacted. The confluence of the elements is guided by a particular *politic*, or ethic of behavior, which is built on trust and works for the public good to ultimately lead to *action*. These dynamics define the CLE theory of change, or RASPPA: Relationships, Assets, Stories, Place, Politic, and Action.

RASPPA: Relationships, Assets, Stories, Place, Politic, and Action

Relationships

The CLE theory of change weaves a collection of layers that interact with elements that are foundational to both understanding and engaging in the process of community change. We glean critical lessons that help us situate the importance of relationships at the center of our thinking on change. Just about everything related to CLE is predicated on the need to invest in building healthy relationships. Without that investment, it is difficult to build trust. Likewise, without trust, it is difficult to build community. Thus, the CLE process begins with the need to build relationships. Pedagogies employed throughout the process lead toward building deeper relationships. Storytelling begets trust; trust begets healthy relationships; healthy relationships beget effective organizations; and effective organizations beget strong communities. Purposeful investment in building relationships is foundational to this work.

The relationship-building efforts during a CLE are supported by the use of Gracious Space. Gracious Space is *a spirit and setting where there is an invitation to the stranger and learning occurs in public*. The Center for Ethical Leadership employs Gracious Spaces to create a climate for deeper listening and understanding. It also helps move relationships beyond the objectives of investment and trust. Investment and trust are critical to the kinds of relationships we want to grow and develop. The growth and development we need best occurs when we trust each other enough, and when we challenge ourselves to live in closer alignment with our life-sustaining principles and values.

Assets

Community leadership teaches us that identifying and building assets is important to understanding and building community. Assets-based development moves us away from deficit-based development that typically crushes the spirit of community. Others involved in human development have observed and commented that when we focus on problems and deficiencies, the problems and deficiencies become larger. When we focus on assets, strengths and solutions, then there is hope. Our communities and the people and families within them need larger and more plentiful assets, strengths, and solutions. By focusing on those community and organizational gifts that already exist, people within those communities and organizations discover their gifts. When we help identify and build the strengths of individuals and communities, everyone feels better about their work. Assets-based community and leadership development inspires people to work together and fosters a spiritual quality that invites community members to the work of community building.

Stories

"I may not own the store," said a CLE participant, "but I totally own my story." An inherent curiosity runs through the work of the CLE. People are curious to know about each other, to know their stories. There is a discipline to this kind of leadership and community development process that requires that individuals find and nurture their own stories. "What's your story?" is a common question posed during the course of a learning exchange. The CLE process encourages everyone to know their individual, their organizational, and their community story. We understand that everyone has a story to tell—even communities have stories to tell—and so the idea of story emerges as an important element in the CLE theory of change and action.

We also know that too often individuals, their organizations, and their communities learn very distorted stories about themselves that have been developed and propagated by those who do not really understand or value them. The role of story during a CLE is both deconstructive and constructive. Participants are invited and challenged to tell their stories, and to examine and decode origins and content. Who did they learn their stories from? Who benefits from their current stories? Who is empowered by them? Are there exceptions to their stories? Are there alternative stories? CLE participants are encouraged to affirm that stories are best when they are owned. And as their most valuable resources they can be re-framed, re-told, and re-shaped to best support their empowerment, agency, and ultimately, their dreams.

Place

Place is a physical location, but it is a process too. The CLE practices place-based teaching, learning, and community and leadership development. Each participant is asked to think about the place they call home, the place that nurtures their curiosity, and the place that inspires their imagination. Place-based pedagogies emerge as prominent, as the CLE process encourages participants to think about the history, the values, and the importance of their communities. Place is important because each community has unique strengths, assets, and gifts, along with the stories that exemplify and illustrate them. Places also have distinct histories and dynamics that need to be understood if efforts to change them are to be successful and just. The understanding of the histories and dynamics of a place is a process worth learning about itself, and that process can only be learned and the skills that support that learning only developed from the real contexts of real places. During a CLE, participants learn about the importance of place within communities that may not even be their own. CLE participants learn about the ecology of place, history, and politics as the necessary conditions to inform the future of their work.

As much as we view community through a critical lens, the CLE similarly encourages us to view community as a place to build, and play, and celebrate. The CLE situates the notion of place at the center of the teaching and learning process. It formalizes community, or place, as a critical ingredient in a theory of change, while also celebrating the rich pageantry of neighborhood and community.

Politic

Behavior intended for the public good characterizes the emerging politic cultivated through CLEs. This is not about "I scratch your back, you scratch mine" behavior; instead, it is about a relational process focused on acting for the betterment of the self, the organization, and the community. Doing the public good is the ethical proposition that guides the workings of the CLE. Politic embodies a kinetic quality, more than potential energy.

Action

A theory of change needs a catalytic quality. Principles that are static and remain in the abstract satisfy the meaning of theory, but a theory in action requires that relationships, assets, stories, and place have movement. Hence, a common question posed during CLEs is, "Does the story have legs?" Stories can possess an aesthetic quality, but in efforts to build community, stories must do more. They must inspire, motivate, and move citizens to act toward the public good.

Building RASPPA

CLEs pose similar questions related to relationships, assets, and place. From a symbolic standpoint reminiscent of the life and culture of South Texas, we use the acronym RASPPA (Relationships, Assets, Stories, Place, Politic, Action); the word *raspa* means "snow cone," a favorite refreshment for local kids and adults alike—and we hope the CLE will be comparably appreciated by all.

The RASPPA model holds our theory of change together. It weaves fundamental principles of relationships, assets, stories, places, politics, and actions with three ecologies of knowing: self, organization, and community. The RASPPA principles are manifest at three levels of development, or ecologies of knowing. The first ecological space is the self, where the most profound development takes place; people change through their interaction with others as they build relationships, develop their assets, share their stories, and learn about their place. The second ecological dimension is the organization; this is where schools, community-based non-profits, universities, or private enterprises grow through the same set of interactions. The third ecological level is the community. The ecologies of knowing interplay fluidly with the principles that define the theory of change. Relationships are built between members of organizations and between members of a community. Stories are shared, nurtured, and utilized for deeper understanding of the self, the organization, and the community. Assets are identified and built through introspective work, through an organization's self-reflection, and/or community dialogues. Each principle and ecology of knowing is situated in a particular place—geographical or metaphorical. As the principles and ecologies of knowing interact, the theory of change is enacted and comes to life.

The integration of these elements along with the five axioms of the CLE value system gives shape to a framework for understanding that pushes us to move our thinking from deficits to assets as a community—a critical prerequisite to beginning to rehabilitate the collective self-esteem of many communities, and especially places that have been marginalized historically. When Llano Grande moved from noting deficits to focusing on assets, the organization better positioned itself to unfetter the immense power of community members to advocate for the bond issues that built new schools and inspired the community to vote to improve the physical infrastructure of the region.

When participants prepare for a Community Learning Exchange, they are asked to think about natural strengths, talents, and skills that are personal, organizational, and community based. "What gifts do you bring to your work in education, leadership, or community development?" is a common question posed. The search for assets encourages participants, organizations, and communities to think critically about the redeeming qualities that exist in every organization and community. The discipline of asset mapping recognizes and honors the work of elders and others who have worked to raise families, create enterprises, and lead institutions in the community. Asset mapping offers opportunities to engage organizations and communities in gaining a deeper understanding of the strengths that exist in community, and it is a requisite step to the process of building the assets identified through mapping. The CLE facilitates asset mapping, and it urges participants to think about culturally responsive and historically appropriate approaches to building those very assets.

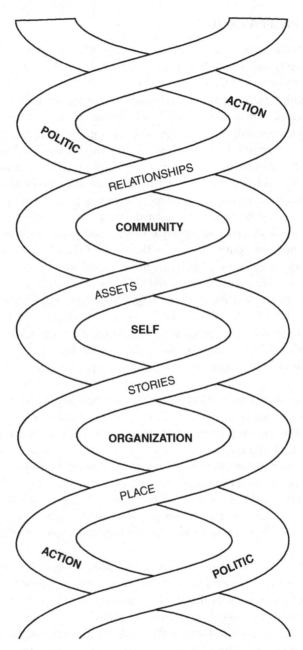

FIGURE 3.1 RASPPA

Bringing RASPPA to Life

A theory of action can be created quite easily. In 1953, U.S. Speaker of the House Sam Rayburn famously said, "Any jackass can kick down a barn door, but it takes a carpenter to build it." Likewise, the real work of the CLE resides in the action. Change requires planning for and attention toward the work that must occur. Time and training are the most often heard variables when talking about change. In our world, this translates to teaching and learning. To create change, there first needs to be a common understanding and language. Normative languages and signature CLE methods and strategies are deliberately taught, not hidden with access only for a privileged few. Next, the procedural elements of how to engage in change processes must be attended to—the process of the Community Learning Exchange must be taught and learned. Finally, change must be monitored, examined, and described with multiple metrics and perspectives and reflected upon from multiple points of view. In the work of the CLE, we use learning methods and strategies, or pedagogies, that are anchored in the CLE axioms, framed by the ecologies of knowing, and lived through RASPPA.

The term that defines the art of teaching is *pedagogy*, which is the method and action of teaching. Oddly enough, there is no word to define the art of learning. Yet there is no value to teaching without learning. Learning is developmental, idiosyncratic, and highly contextualized. That is, learning takes place at different times for different people in a variety of settings. Place, space, style, personal beliefs, experiences, and interests all intersect simultaneously. There is an art in developing awareness and critical consciousness as well as building agency at the various levels of the ecologies of knowing (self, community, and organization). This is dynamic-critical pedagogy. This does not separate learning from teaching, and vice versa. We do not want to neglect other values that support the learning and development process, nor can we set aside other elements of the CLE theory of change. Teaching and learning during a CLE must honor the full context of community and the human experiences that take place within them—place, space, family, community, policy, history, politics, play. These are important and must be attended to along with other elements valuable to informing understanding and change.

We have learned from those great educational minds who saw learning as both a cognitive and social endeavor. The canonical thinkers and the wise elders and youth in our own families teach us that the cognitive development is no more important than social and socio-cultural experiences. What a person already knows, has experienced, and likes all shapes how they will make meaning of the world. This hinges on relationships among individuals, the places they reside and work, and the families and communities they rely on. In the CLE process, deep and caring relationships matter most.

PART II

The Work

DRAWING 2 Artwork by Mónica Valadez.

Source: Mónica Valadez. Used with permission.

4

STORYTELLING

Stories of Impact

Storytelling in Public

The Community Learning Exchange changes people's lives. It has changed our lives: as sons, brothers, fathers, professors, friends, and agents for community change. Just as we have changed personally, we have also helped change the organizations we work in, and we have changed the communities where we live. This chapter explores the three ecologies of knowing—self, organization, community—through stories that are personal. We tell stories that explore the self, that delve into the identity of an organization, and that focus on community impact. Three of the stories are told in the first person, because they are stories we experienced personally. We lived these stories. We own them. They originate within us, so they are more than an intellectual exercise, just as the CLE is personal, as much as it is an intellectual challenge. The stories dig into the roots of the CLE. They help make meaning of our experience, and they describe the agency that is manifest through the work. The stories illustrate that this work has to be lived, because by living it the work becomes more full, and more sustainable.

Storytelling in the CLE context is more than an element in the theory of change. It is a critical pedagogical tool, as we employ it as an important part of building the self, organizations, and communities. Those who participate in CLEs will quickly be faced with the quintessential CLE question, What's your story? The invitation is fundamental to build relationships and to build the curriculum and the setting for learning about the topic at hand through our lived experiences. The storytelling process invites CLE participants to think within their lived experience, while providing the space to expand it in a socio-cognitive manner. Through conversations and sharing stories, participants build the skills to name their lived experiences in the social world, the cognitive world, and through dialogue in a relational world. This moves storytelling from a monologue to a space of sharing, interaction, and conversation. The dialogue takes place introspectively, within local teams, and with the community at large. This dynamic is embedded throughout the life cycle of the broader CLE pedagogy.

We invite the reader to consider local stories of assets, struggles, celebrations, hopes, and visions that inform the survival and success in your community. The process of storytelling sets the stage for a specific brand of learning as we begin to remember, reflect, and re-author our own story. The following sections take us into the actions employed at the CLE to guide participants through this learning, meaning-making, and knowledge-creation process. The following stories are told through personal voices and aim to characterize the essence of the CLE experience.

A Story of Guidance and Development

Told by Miguel Guajardo

My two sons grew up playing, exploring, and following each other around the house. They explored their environment all day, until they fell asleep from the exhaustion of play. Their world started within the four walls of the house, and it grew when they ventured to the backyard, where the garden became the farm. Their garden bore fruit, which they patiently awaited and then ate off the vine, as if they scavenged off the natural vegetation. When tomato plants were ready for harvest, they ate them too. The garden became a place for snacking. Their expanded world contained a place where they dug for dinosaur fossils as they enacted their roles as paleontologists. They were into everything, because their environment offered everything. They went on expeditions to explore the next pot of gold or worked to invent the newest toy that would transform the world. They explored, created stories, shared experiences, laughed, and played all day. When their mother or I called them into the house to eat, their response would be, "We will eat out here. We are dinosaurs that live in the wild! And we will wash our hands with the water hose." Their exploration nurtured in them the ability to negotiate the imaginary with the necessary.

At the end of the workday, when I arrived home from work, they ran to the door to greet me. They are three years apart but were equally interested in learning about my day and really everything that I experienced outside the home. My older son, the more verbal of the two, was always the first to ask, "How was your day, Papi? Tell me everything, everything, everything . . ." He did this as he waved his hands roundly, requesting that I tell all. My younger son, who was naturally shyer, mimicked the older one's request with similar excitement and hand gestures. I willingly obliged, as I became the messenger for the dealings of the outside world.

Theory in Action

In the next few chapters, we explore and learn more about how a CLE is framed and how a rhythm is developed for it. As you will learn, whether through the planning of a CLE or experiencing one, the goal of the CLE is to work toward positioning people in places where they will be successful. This begins prior to the start of the CLE, and we have found that the best engagement practices begin with the invitation. The best invitations are personal, informative, and, well, inviting.

We must be committed to making our invitations authentic, the topic or issue relevant, and the engagement process dynamic. We have found that our invitations for CLEs are most authentic when we welcome the wisdom and gifts of participants. We have also found that the topic or issues of a CLE will be relevant when they are shaped with participants, rather than brought to them without their input and collaboration. We have also found that the engagement process is dynamic when we interact with the intention of building relationships first, and engaging in learning tasks after those relationships are first honored. In that spirit, we invite you to bring your experiences of living and learning in community. In the next section, you will learn more about the Community Learning Exchange from stories of impacts on individuals, organizations, and communities. Sharing stories is the foundation of our relationships. Stories are how we communicate our experiences and our histories. Stories are also what allow us to view and understand our experiences. As you read these stories, ask yourself how you can take what you learn to better honor the spirit and power of place as well as the wisdom of people in your own communities. How can you use the five axioms of the Community Learning Exchange, the ecologies of knowing, and the theory of change in action so that you can better understand and engage in your own collective change efforts? Through our stories of the Community Learning Exchange, we invite you to dream about a new story for yourself, your family, your organization, and your community.

References and Further Readings

Alinsky, S. (1969). *Reveille for radicals*. New York, NY: Vintage Books.

Block, P. (2009). *Community: The structure of belonging*. San Francisco, CA: Berrett-Koehler.

Dewey, J. (1963). *Experience and education*. New York: Collier Books.

Guajardo, M. (2009). Collective leadership: Practice, theory, and praxis. *Journal of Leadership Studies, 3*(2), 70–73.

Guajardo, M., Guajardo, F., & Casaperalta, E. (2008). Transformative education: Chronicling a pedagogy for social change. *Anthropology and Education Quarterly, 39*(1), 3–22.

Habermas, J. (1984). *The theory of communicative action* (Vol. 2, T. McCarthy, Trans.). Boston, MA: Beacon Press.

McKnight, J., & Block, P. (2010). *The abundant community: Awakening the power of families and neighborhoods*. San Francisco, CA: Berrett-Koehler.

PHOTO 4.1 The Guajardo boys telling stories (Emiliano, Javier, and Miguel). Photographer: Joyce Guajardo.

During the course of the day, my wife facilitated the exploratory process. She created and nurtured the necessary structure to keep the children focused, the clean environment to keep them safe, and the stimulating opportunities for asking questions and inviting conversation. Exploring and creating stories was the charge throughout the day. Parental roles were reversed when necessary, as my wife also explored into the world of work, visiting friends, grandparents, or new places to expand learning. As parents, we became scouts, in perpetual search of new places to tap as educational settings. Mother also became an explorer and messenger of new experiences, and the daily roles and responsibilities were always negotiated. The children witnessed the negotiated process, so they learned and emulated the process as they played and created roles and responsibilities for each other, for friends, for cousins, or for anyone who visited.

Field trips were critical to the learning experience. They augmented the home experiences and allowed for further research. This spirit of learning resonates with us when we think of the spirit of children within the learning process. Particularly instructive is their innocence in not discriminating while remaining open and ready to embrace the new experiences of people they trust. Trust requires we be in relationship with them, a reality that is at the core of social learning theory. Children model for us the necessary condition of openness to new ideas, new practices, and new conversations for growth and development.

This theory and practice as parents, teachers, and community activists informs the meaning-making process at the Community Learning Exchange. Though the context, lessons learned, and lived experiences are complex and at times intense, the meaning-making process is accessible. It must be developmental, dynamic, and reachable by all participants if we are to invite the diversity we value as part of the processes of learning and making meaning. Diversity is in people, in the thinking, in the ability and experience, and in the meaning making. We invite meaningful conversations and thoughts, and augment them with spirited experiences marked by an intensity of engagement. The experiences allow for active learning through a process that pronounces the stories and realities of participants.

The boys' story is important as an example of how the ontology of the CLE has informed a way for raising children. This process is neither simple nor easy; it is filled with tension that creates deep learning. I can see the tension that would escalate into hostility if we tried to raise our children within this espoused system with traditional power dynamics in place. The boys grew up in a collective decision-making environment. When opportunities presented themselves and when non-high-stake issues were deliberated, they were part of the decision-making process. As parents we protect our children, first and foremost, and when appropriate, we also use life as pedagogy for our children's development; we work to find those opportunities as often as possible. When liberating our schema from the traditional roles and responsibilities of unidirectional power, moving to a relational power dynamic and educating children in a collaborative setting, the learning opportunities for children and parents become abundant. The level of awareness and the engagement become relational and pedagogical.

Clearly the parent maintains the responsibility for the child throughout, and the space nurtured for collective development, decision making, and education is consistently being negotiated. The growth of both parents and children is always developing within an interdependent setting. This level of awareness has informed the way we have grown as parents, as educators, and as citizens in our democratic society. The learning process within this context is critically important to our children as they grow and develop into young adults in our community. It has been a privilege to witness the way their landscape for development has grown from the backyard, to the neighborhood block, and into the neighborhood. They have nurtured the relationship building process with their friends at school, within the neighborhood, and with their relatives who may live across town or across the state. Their ability to navigate relationships has also contributed to their academic and intellectual development, as they grow into young men within this CLE culture and with these axioms as their guiding way of life. They have been able to navigate their young lives with hope and the understanding that living by these rules does not always guarantee success, but it does provide an opportunity to expand their understanding of the world around them in a dignified way.

I share these ontological principles to highlight the utility and transference of the CLE values, axioms, strategies, and culture from the space we share with strangers to the space we nurture within our own personal lives at home, within our organizations, and with our communities of practice. My communities of practice are embedded in places that have situated their presence within and beyond my household. This mentoring and coaching model for development of a citizen within my household also holds true when preparing and mentoring graduate students within my institution. The relational process of development and scaffolding is useful when nurturing the imagination and agency of students in search of a different way of learning, acting, and living. This is apparent in teachers working to expand their craft, just as it is evident with PhD students working on dissertations. The collective nature of teaching, learning, and leading is clear and present as they matriculate through their exploratory process to the completion of their work and the expansion of their imagination. The CLE culture is present as they organize, develop, and host writing teams for themselves and their colleagues.

The CLE as a structure and process is not the end of the work, but it is the work, the product, and the strategy for living life in a relational and fulfilling manner.

Uncaptioned Pictures

Told by Matt Militello

In late 2014, my father-in-law died. At the young age of 71, John Edward Goldner left a large number of family and friends behind. As is the case with the death of a loved one, there is a process of loss, sadness, remembrance, and healing that people go through. However, for my wife and her sister, there was also a business side that was unexpectedly distracting and interrupted the process for them. When we gathered for funeral proceedings and to say goodbye, an awkwardness was present. Fortunately, we had a knight-errant in the form of a high school student.

★ ★ ★ ★ ★ ★

Liz (my wife and partner) and I have four beautiful young boys: Dominic, Luke, Gabriel, and Oscar. Three of my sons have been involved in the Community Learning Exchange work in a number of ways. At home we practice sharing at mealtime, where we ask each individual to reflect on something they are thankful for or a specific question that is important at the moment. The kids are comfortable with aspects of sharing because of the modeling that takes place by my wife and me, but also because the three older boys have attended national CLEs over the years. In fact, Dominic has been a core member of the national CLE team since he was in the 8th grade.

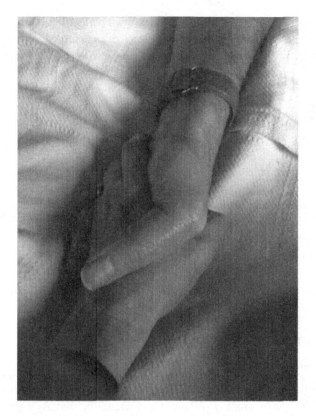

PHOTO 4.2 Liz and her father holding hands days preceding his death. Photographer Elizabeth Militello.

When the original funding for the Kellogg Leadership for Community Change (KLCC) was completed, a number of the national organizers made a pitch to the Kellogg Foundation to continue the work in a different format. While the KLCC work focused on the development of community-based individuals, the CLE would charter unfamiliar territory by engaging in learning exchanges with teams from around the country on a specific topic. The idea was that a community university—where the curriculum and teaching and learning strategies are influenced by the wisdom of the people and power of place—can be grounds to learn, exchange ideas, and develop community leaders in order to make meaningful, thoughtful changes in their communities.

During the KLCC work (2003–2010), I was a member of the national evaluation team led by my mentor, Dr. Maenette Benham, who would become the founding dean of the Hawaiʻinuiākea School of Hawaiian Knowledge at the University of Hawaii. In her new role, she was unable to continue the intense work of being an active member of the national team and the leader of the evaluation team. Maenette graciously offered my name as an able contributor to the next iteration of the work.

I took the responsibility humbly and relied on the mentorship I received to make the first important decision: making the evaluation of the CLE participatory and engaging where a set of strategies would be employed that allowed CLE participants and the CLE leadership team to learn from one another—collaboratively and organically. To begin this process, I asked others to be a part of the evaluation team. In 2010, I asked Chris Janson to work with me and we identified two youths who we would name as evaluators to help us with the work: Emiliano Guajardo was a sophomore in high school and Dominic Militello, my son, was in seventh grade. Each became a valuable member of the CLE national evaluation team.

I provide this background as context for a story about Dominic and his engagement with our theory of change (RASPPA) and specific CLE pedagogies in a time of pain and suffering.

★ ★ ★ ★ ★ ★

In preparation for the viewing, Dominic and our family were helping my wife find and paste photos of John on poster boards. The intent was for visitors to see John through the ages. Liz was confronted with question after question from our boys:

- "Where was this taken?"
- "Who is that with Grandpa?"
- "What is Grandpa doing in that photo?"
- "How old was Grandpa then?"

and so on. In many cases, Liz did not know how to respond. There were so many pictures, so many experiences, friends, and places. While the photos themselves told a story, the fact that so many photos were caption-less left many stories untold.

Later that evening, a local host team was created around the topic of the "uncaptioned pictures." Dominic, Liz, and I had a meaningful conversation about the photos, what was still untold, unknown. We asked Liz what we should expect the next day at the viewing, and she described the traditional process of a visitation. Dominic and I knew at that moment what kinds of experiences would be more helpful and eloquent to the visitors that would come to honor John Goldner. Moreover, these experiences would fill in the missing stories we ached for. Dominic shared with his mom about Circle. He described what a Circle was and how he experienced them at national CLEs. He then went on to make a pitch to have a Circle for his grandfather! It was incredible. It was a clarifying moment for me about Dominic's development and integration of the CLE work. For his mom, it was a reversal of learning roles—Dominic was passionately making the case for creating an experience that would honor his grandfather and invite voices of the visitors—the keepers of many of the stories—to actively engage in the visitation. Rather than keep the visitors passive, Dominic suggested that we engage them in a formalized way. Liz agreed.

Dominic knew he had work to do. Engaging in a process of experiential learning takes preparation and staging. Dominic and I first needed to find a space and create the right kind of setup. We went to a restaurant across the street from the funeral home and reserved a back room. We spoke with the manager and set the room up as a horseshoe. Dominic then left to spend time in his grandfather's basement; he needed to find a talking piece—the symbol granting participants their turn to talk—that would be used in Circle.

Hours before the Circle, Dominic moved his preparation from our local network to a national network. He sent text messages to Chris, Miguel, and Francisco—ideas about the guiding questions for the Circle were discussed, and words of support and encouragement were sent Dominic's way (see Photos 4.3 and 4.4).

Approximately 40 people gathered for food and conversation at the restaurant that evening. Dominic stood and addressed the crowd:

> We want to thank everyone for coming. This has been a difficult time for all of us. I would like for us to gather and sit together, in a circle, and share stories about my grandfather. My three brothers, my three cousins, and I want to add captions to the photos of our grandfather and we believe you are the people who can help us.

With that cue, the people gathered in Circle. Dominic provided a brief overview of the Circle process, the history of Circle (indigenous storytelling), and some ground rules associated with Circle (e.g., the opportunity to pass without speaking). Dominic described the talking piece—a model car he retrieved from his grandpa's basement. He told the participants how his relationship with his grandfather was amplified by their mutual love for cars. Dominic then posed a guiding question—"What is a powerful memory of my grandfather you hold?"—and then he passed the model car to his left.

★ ★ ★ ★ ★ ★

This is a story of the power of learning from, and being led by, youth. This is a story of finding the time and space in the midst of sadness and chaos to remind us that there is a healing power in storytelling. This is a story of the developmental qualities in relationships between a mother and a son. Liz's reaction to the Circle during a debriefing session Dominic and I had with her was complex. She began

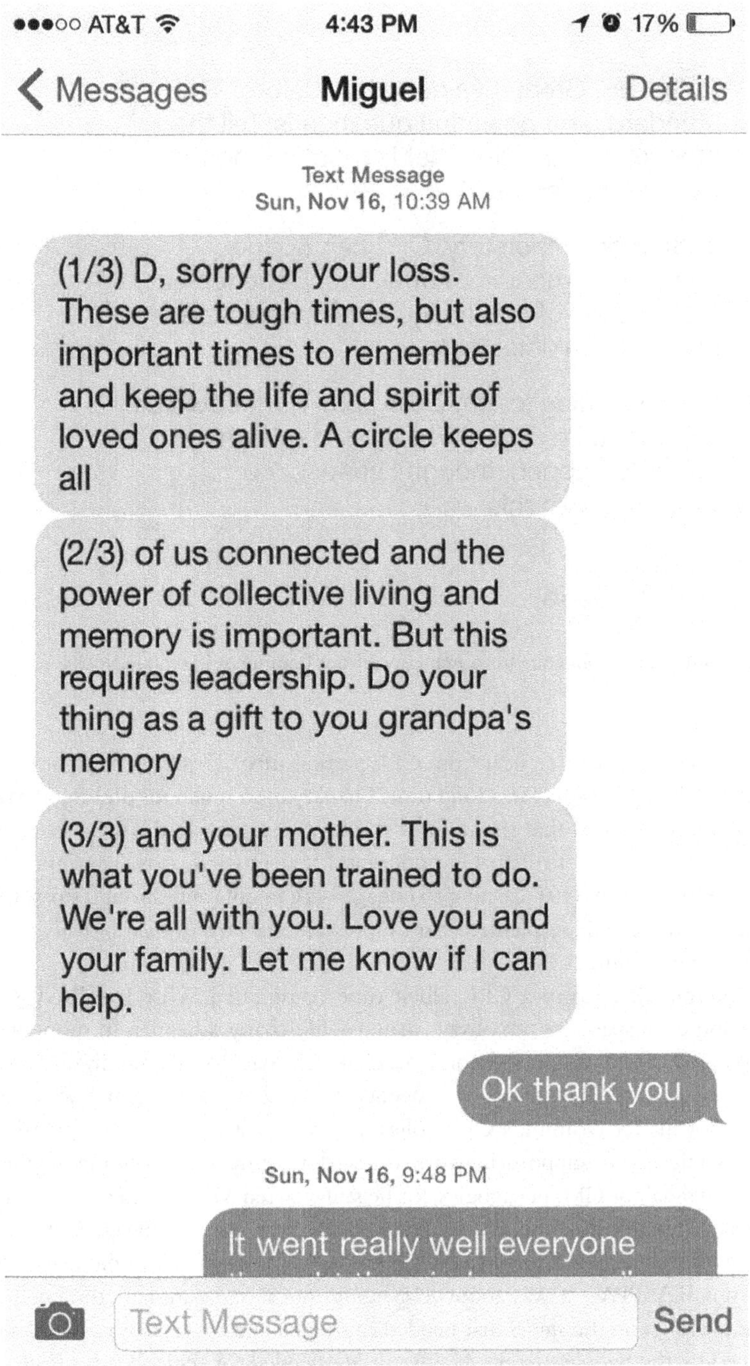

Text Message
Sun, Nov 16, 10:39 AM

(1/3) D, sorry for your loss. These are tough times, but also important times to remember and keep the life and spirit of loved ones alive. A circle keeps all

(2/3) of us connected and the power of collective living and memory is important. But this requires leadership. Do your thing as a gift to you grandpa's memory

(3/3) and your mother. This is what you've been trained to do. We're all with you. Love you and your family. Let me know if I can help.

Ok thank you

Sun, Nov 16, 9:48 PM

It went really well everyone

📷   Text Message   Send

PHOTO 4.3 Correspondence with Miguel about Circle

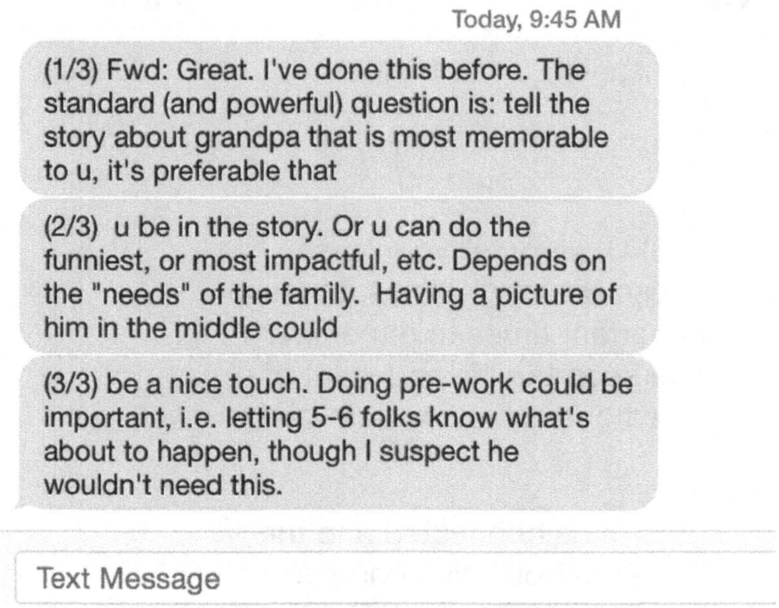

Today, 9:45 AM

(1/3) Fwd: Great. I've done this before. The standard (and powerful) question is: tell the story about grandpa that is most memorable to u, it's preferable that

(2/3) u be in the story. Or u can do the funniest, or most impactful, etc. Depends on the "needs" of the family. Having a picture of him in the middle could

(3/3) be a nice touch. Doing pre-work could be important, i.e. letting 5-6 folks know what's about to happen, though I suspect he wouldn't need this.

Text Message

PHOTO 4.4 Correspondence from Francisco about framing guiding questions for Circle

with something we often hear from CLE participants:"That was the most power-ful experience I have had in a long time.Thank you so much for pushing for this." Liz also felt ashamed that she did not think of engaging in this kind of experi-ence herself.We had to help Liz understand that moving away from normative practices is difficult.That learning to engage with people and through story, while ancient in design and implementation, represents *new ways of knowing and doing* for many in communities.

Dominic engaged in a CLE, albeit time constrained. What I realized is that time and even space do not always matter—life changes happen in spontaneous and unpredictable ways. It did not matter, though, that all of the family and friends were not present—but those who needed to be there that evening were there. It did not matter Dominic's CLE colleagues were not present, as a network was quickly engaged to support the work.It also did not matter that Dominic did not have a manual for CLE pedagogies, for he still enacted Meaningful Conversations, critical self-reflection, and Circle. What did matter was his engagement of the axioms and theory of change that CLE has instilled in him. Dominic led a Circle that was RASPPA—it was about *relationships* (local and national), the *assets* that were present, and the *stories* that needed to be told and heard. It was *set* in a place defined by the people present. It was a *politic* needed for the collective souls, and he did so by taking *action*.

PHOTO 4.5 Grandchildren of John Goldner. Photographer: Matthew Militello.

Although I am uncertain of many things in life, I am certain of a few: I had the privilege of being introduced to this work and now have the privilege of continuing the work with my children. By directly involving, modeling, and encouraging this work, my children will develop their own normative practice—*a new way of knowing and doing*—that will surface when needed. We must always be open to learning from everywhere and anytime; as Cervantes wrote in *Don Quixote*: "Fortune always leaves a door open in adversity."

PHOTO 4.6 Liz holding the talking piece with Oscar and Dominic in the background. Photographer: Matthew Militello.

The mystery of the uncaptioned pictures was not resolved through a prolonged search but rather an invitation and graciousness of offering and listening to story—an invitation that was shepherded by a young man. By the time this book is published, Dominic will be in college, out of our house, and in a new community—a community that Dominic will help engage in the work of the CLE, so that its experiences, its pictures, are captioned.

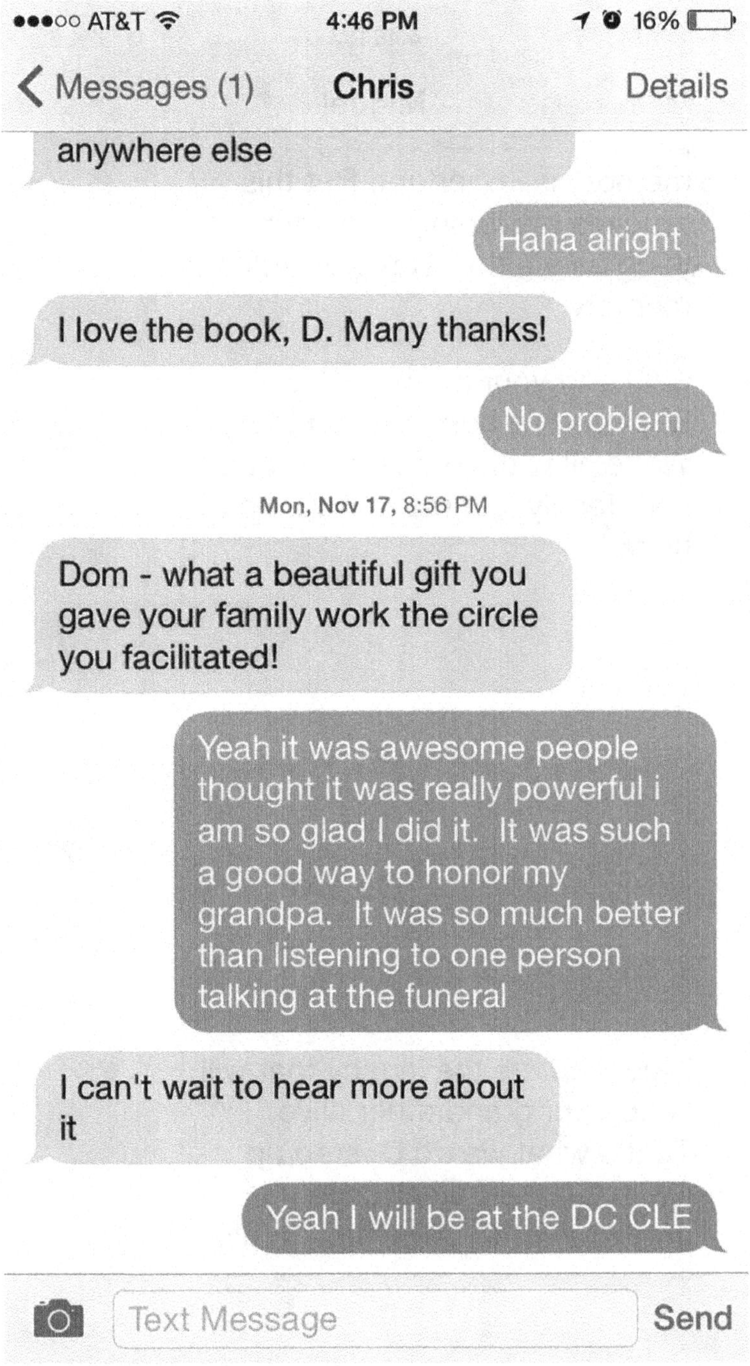

anywhere else

Haha alright

I love the book, D. Many thanks!

No problem

Mon, Nov 17, 8:56 PM

Dom - what a beautiful gift you gave your family work the circle you facilitated!

Yeah it was awesome people thought it was really powerful i am so glad I did it. It was such a good way to honor my grandpa. It was so much better than listening to one person talking at the funeral

I can't wait to hear more about it

Yeah I will be at the DC CLE

 Text Message   Send

PHOTO 4.7 Correspondence with Chris reflecting on the Circle

memory is important. But this requires leadership. Do your thing as a gift to you grandpa's memory

(3/3) and your mother. This is what you've been trained to do. We're all with you. Love you and your family. Let me know if I can help.

Ok thank you

Sun, Nov 16, 9:48 PM

It went really well everyone thought the circle was really cool and it was a great way to remember my grandfather.

Sun, Nov 16, 10:54 PM

Nice! You are the legacy that will keep your grandfather alive. That's what we do D, step up when we are called. Love you and your family. Big hugs to all.

 Text Message   Send

PHOTO 4.8 Correspondence with Miguel reflecting on the Circle

Asset Mapping and Development

Told by Francisco Guajardo

The Community Learning Exchange encourages asset identification and asset building that are personal, organizational, and communal. The integration of the theory of change elements gives shape to a framework for understanding that pushes us to move our thinking from deficits to assets as a community. This integration is a critical prerequisite to begin to rehabilitate the collective self-esteem of many communities, especially those that have been marginalized historically. The Llano Grande Center was created with a consciousness to identify and build assets, and because of that it was able to advocate for bond issues to build new schools and to inspire the community to vote on improving the physical infrastructure of the region.

When participants prepare for a learning exchange, they are asked to think about natural strengths, talents, and skills that are personal, organizational, and community based. "What gifts do you bring to your work in education, leadership, or community development?" is a common question posed. The search for assets encourages participants, organizations, and communities to think critically about redeeming qualities that exist in every organization and community. The discipline of asset mapping recognizes and honors the work of elders and others who work to raise families, create enterprises, and lead institutions in the community. Asset mapping offers opportunities to engage organizations and communities in gaining a deeper understanding of the strengths that exist in community, and it is a requisite step to the process of building the assets identified through mapping. The CLE facilitates asset mapping, and it urges participants to think about culturally responsive and historically appropriate approaches to building those very assets.

An example of asset mapping and asset development transpired in rural South Texas as a result of a partnership between the local high school and the community-based organization, the Llano Grande Center. Students in social studies classes at the high school engaged in an elaborate asset mapping process where they walked the streets of their hometown going door to door to take stock of assets extant within homes and neighborhoods. A traditional market analysis of this community would suggest that it is economically impoverished; because scant industry can be found in the town, it exists in financial distress and without ample opportunity. Through the asset mapping exercise, however, students found a different story. As they traversed the streets of their hometown with clipboard and asset inventory in hand, students documented the strengths that local folks wanted to share. In the end, the assets most reported included (a) stories people told about themselves, their families, or their home town and (b) the use of the Spanish language. The conventional view that proficiency with the English language holds the highest value in community life was challenged by this asset map exercise, as community members viewed proficiency in Spanish equally valuable. The results revealed what community members deemed important, a way of thinking that then shaped a community and economic development agenda that placed the community assets of (a) stories and (b) Spanish at the center of strategic planning.

Youth and adults at Llano Grande prepared to create two community-based enterprises that have been useful on many levels. They first secured support to build the infrastructure for a digital storytelling business which would assist nonprofit organizations, educators, and students in the process of crafting stories through the utilizations of digital technologies. Teachers now use digital storytelling to reimagine the way they plan lessons, the way they teach, and the way they assess student performance. Organizations use the process to articulate the history, purpose, and identity of the organization, which they typically tell through Internet and other publishable media. High school students employ storytelling skills to enhance their college preparation and application process. Understanding the mechanics of how to tell a story benefits students as they craft college admissions essays, compete for scholarships, and gain a deeper understanding of their goals and dreams. Beyond the benefit to teachers, organizations, and students, the digital storytelling work has also generated local employment opportunities that respect local strengths.

Opportunities stemming from the local use of Spanish yielded results similar to those from the local storytelling capacity. Youth and adults again partnered to build support to create a Spanish Language Immersion Institute, through which they recruited medical profession workers, educators, and nonprofit workers. They developed a cottage industry, wherein they recruited monolingual Spanish speaking elderly couples willing to participate in the Spanish immersion work by housing participants who came from other South Texas communities and from different parts of the country. Participants engaged in Spanish conversations during breakfast, dinner, and evening social activities while they followed a daytime curriculum focused on building Spanish language skills through conversational and other cultural strategies. *Plática*, or a culturally nuanced conversation, was employed as an important language learning strategy. Community youth worked closely with teachers from the local schools and the elders who provided housing to deliver wide-ranging instructional opportunities that tapped academic, social, and culturally relevant pedagogies. The impact can be measured through the creation of culturally supportive employment opportunities and the immersion institute has provided a valuable service to those interested in learning the Spanish language. In short, we reframed how we viewed ourselves as assets, and consequently created community change.

Cultivating Communities for CLEs

Told by Chris Janson

Our local Community Learning Exchange work in Jacksonville, Florida, grew from the national CLEs that members of our local planning team attended. After I had participated in my first national CLE in Washington, DC, I felt profoundly changed by what I experienced there and returned to Jacksonville and my university community eager to share the new understandings of collective leadership I had developed through the stories, strategies, and pedagogies I had witnessed and shared.

Through my continued involvement in the national CLEs, I began to recognize and understand how the axioms of the CLE had profound implications, not just for my teaching and work with students both in the university and area public schools, but also for who I am within the context of my family and my community. For instance, bringing to life the axiom that the *crossing of boundaries is essential to enrich learning* led to profound changes in how I structured my graduate courses. It was no longer enough to rely on academic sources within the silo of the university to help us make meaning about collective leadership. Instead, I began to situate our learning about collective leadership within the context of our community by creating opportunities and spaces to learn not just from the scholarship of our discipline, but from community members, activists, and organizers who were living it every day in their neighborhoods and organizations.

Still further, when we met on campus, I invited students to bring along family and community members interested in community leadership and development. These new voices provided invaluable perspectives, strategies, and stories that enhanced our collective learning while energizing our spirit. As an example, during a Circle, each person was invited to reflect on how we might potentially transform our current roles to make our community healthier and safer. One guest hesitantly shared that she did not feel positioned to impact community in her work because she was "only a hair stylist." In response, others in the room encouraged her to reimagine her narrative by engaging in *conversation and dialogue* through sharing a story Myles Horton once told about Highlander efforts to mobilize voter registration among African American citizens in the rural South during the 1950s. While working from another axiom of the CLE, *that people closest to the issues are best situated to know answers to local concerns*, residents helped the Highlander team identify community members who were at the epicenter of community discourse and thus best positioned to inform potential voters and mobilize them to register to vote. These citizens were hair stylists and barbers. Highlander then worked with these hair stylists and barbers to help them understand how they could use their gifts to transform their community's political and social circumstances. Before leaving class that night, our guest shared with the rest of us that she had never before felt so hopeful and empowered. What she provided was a beautiful illustration of another axiom: *that hope and change are built on assets and dreams of locals and their communities.*

This axiom of hope and change emerging from the assets and dreams of people in communities provoked more reflection on my knowledge and understanding of the Jacksonville community and the importance of examining it for previously under-recognized assets and strengths. It was through my relationship with a young community educator, activist, and hip-hop artist named Travis Pinckney that I learned about a community asset that provided the local context, flavor, and expressions of work that mirrored some of the important elements of the CLE. In doing so, Travis helped introduce and welcome me into a community that would be another great inspiration for me, a small neighborhood church shepherded by Travis's uncle, Pastor Rod Pinckney.

At that time, Travis and I were developing college-transition curriculum based on hip-hop narratives for students in urban neighborhoods as well as the installation of a recording studio within a middle school. The idea for the after-school hip-hop program was born from my first visit to Murray Hill during a youth-focused service that generously provided space and opportunity for their youth parishioners to worship through hip-hop music and dance. Through conversations I had with Pastor Rod Pinckney, I knew that it was not an easy decision that the elders of the church made to allow the introduction of a youth culture medium that many of them had previously associated only with negative and harmful messages about drugs, sex, and violence. Yet, their reservations notwithstanding, the elders of the church and Pastor Rod recognized that sharing space and power with youth would not only help support the development of those youth, but it could also serve to reinvigorate the church and all of its parishioners by inviting new ideas and approaches for worship and celebrations of life. During my first experience in Murray Hill Christ Community Church, the energy of their faith community and the graciousness in which they were providing substantial leadership opportunities to youth encouraged Travis and I to apply elements of that model and approach within a public school and, unbeknownst to us at the time, cultivated the soil in which our local CLE work would grow.

Just as I was learning about community development efforts through the practices and approaches of the congregation of Murray Hill Christ Community Church, I was also sharing with Travis and his uncle things I was learning and applying from the national CLEs and the thinkers and activists who influenced them. When we would talk about how we wanted our work within Jacksonville to be more centered around the strengths, assets, and gifts of the youth and families learning and living in them, I would share the powerful stories I had learned and witnessed from the work of Miguel and Francisco Guajardo through the Llano Grande Center and within their local communities. We also formed a study group and together began reading works by and about Myles Horton and the Highlander Folk School. In doing so, we also began to strategize how we could apply more of what we were learning to our work in schools, the university, and the church.

It was through our collective learning and strategizing that Pastor Rod, Travis, and I realized that while the ways we engaged and worked in community were changing, we were changing, too. When we would share with each other our particular work, community, and family challenges, we increasingly anchored our conversations in the language and practices of the CLE. When one of us was facing difficulty building community somewhere, another would ask would ask, "How are you attempting to create Gracious Space?" When we were seeking counsel regarding individuals in our lives who were experiencing challenging problems, we would ask, "How can you help that person shift their narrative, their story, from the problem to solutions?" And, just as with the hair stylist in the collective leadership course, we would challenge each other to name the gifts we were bringing to our work in education, leadership, and community development.

We became much closer in the process and our relationships with each other became stronger. And within the context of our closer relationships, we strove to be very intentional about something I had heard Miguel Guajardo say, "We strive to create Gracious Space not with the goal of becoming safe and comfortable with each other, but in order to become safe and secure enough in our relationships so we can better challenge ourselves to become better friends, better neighbors, better parents, and better change agents."

As much as I would share with Travis and Pastor Rod the things I learned and experienced at the national CLEs, I also recognized that CLEs have to be experienced in order to deeply understand both their process and their power to facilitate change. Soon the opportunity came to bring Travis and another community educator with me, as a Jacksonville team, to a CLE thought leader meeting at one of the places we by then considered to be holy ground for community change work—the Highlander Center. The three of us drove up from Jacksonville to Highlander in New Market, Tennessee, using the time to share our intentions for what we wanted and needed to experience there. Most importantly, we discussed what we wanted to bring back to Jacksonville from our experience that we could transform into action.

It was at Highlander where Travis was first able to experience the powerful dynamic of a CLE and the elements of the theory of change that had developed around them—the central role relationships play in precipitating and supporting development; the emphasis on individual and community assets; the importance of sharing and honoring each other's individual and community stories; and the importance of place. During those four days, my friendship with Travis grew even closer, and a huge part of that growth came from Travis meeting and building new relationships with many of the people he had only known from my stories until that point. Likewise, others who were at Highlander and had heard my stories about Travis were able to meet him, hear his stories, and experience his gifts.

We felt challenged, renewed, and changed at Highlander. For Travis and our other Jacksonville friend and ally in the work, we spent the return car ride home talking about how we were going to respond to the call Francisco Guajardo invited us to reflect on during the closing Circle. Retelling a story, from a similar Learning Circle years before at Highlander, he had heard from the cook over the weekend, Francisco challenged us by recalling what Myles Horton had told Rosa

Parks when she went to see him to share, and learn, and strategize shortly before the Montgomery Bus Boycott: "So Rosa, what are you going to do when you get back home?" Francisco recounted this line and told us that Rosa replied, "I don't know. But I know I've got to do something." During that nine hour car ride back, Travis and I decided together that *our something* would be to extend and adapt the work of the CLE within our communities in Jacksonville.

Our first local CLE in Jacksonville, Florida, was held during spring 2012. That daylong CLE was originally conceived as an opportunity for doctoral students to put into practice, to experience, some of the ideas, concepts, and theories they were learning in a course on collective leadership alongside community members from diverse cultural backgrounds. The focus and theme of this CLE (like the next two held during 2012) was collective leadership itself. This was a purposeful decision made with the intention of deepening community understanding and engagement in the work of collective leadership. Travis, Pastor Rod, and I planned, organized, and facilitated the initial Jacksonville CLE. Importantly, it was not held on the university campus, but within Murray Hill Christ Community Church.

These three initial Jacksonville CLEs were rich and fruitful in many beautiful ways. With each one, our planning team grew. We added master's and doctoral students from the University of North Florida, public school educators, high school students, community activists, artists, and musicians. With each new member of our team, we strove to invite each other's gifts to our process, pedagogy, and curriculum. In doing so, we experienced firsthand how the interplay among elements of the CLE Theory of Change (RASPPA) informs and generates additional layers of meaning to the others. For instance, from the musicality of many of our team members, as well as the deep musical traditions and history of Jacksonville, grew an emphasis on music as a pedagogical tool used in each of our CLEs. These musical assets among our team lead us to take action to seek other ways music had been utilized in our city and region to instill hope and inspire. For instance, the song "Lift Ev'ry Voice and Sing," which has come to be known as the "Negro National Anthem," was written by Jacksonville natives James Weldon and John Rosamond Johnson. This extraordinary song would eventually and fittingly be featured prominently in our first national CLE, which was constructed, in part, around stories of the moral courage of our community's early civil rights activists.

During the next few years, the development of our CLE team continued to be supported by our interaction and participation with the National CLEs. We would send teams to each of the national CLEs with the intent to not only bring our experiences, wisdom, and strategies, but also to return with additional perspectives and approaches around the topics of those CLEs; as importantly, we also sought to return with the rhythms, pedagogies, and planning processes and approaches to inform and improve our own.

With the support of the national team and our brothers and sisters in CLE communities across the country, the next iteration of our local CLEs shifted to focus on community challenges. In each case, the organizing theme or issue of our CLEs has been generated by the conditions and desires of the community or neighborhoods and the people within them. In doing so, we work with those community members who *are closest to the issues* to shape the CLE topic and recruit participants, as well as to identify, select, and develop the pedagogies. All of our preparatory work with community members is purposed toward developing a process that holds the most potential to create the best conditions for community members to share their respective experiences with the problem or challenge; engage in collective analyses of the problem or challenge; and then learn from each other's wisdom and apply each other's gifts so they can begin to construct useful approaches and strategies in order to address the problem or challenge.

During this time we have also learned to apply CLE pedagogies, as well as elements of the CLE theory of change and its axioms, to our public schools and universities in Jacksonville. For example, within the public schools, we focused our efforts to rethink and reimagine "parent and family engagement" by recasting traditional, didactic "Parent Information Nights" that have historically been conducted by high school counselors across the country. Rather than the traditional approach in which college application information is dumped on parents rendered passive in the process, we developed what are essentially condensed, three-hour-long micro-CLEs, which we refer to as "Family Wisdom Exchanges." We co-develop these sessions with students and their families and structure them with the dynamic-critical pedagogies of the CLE. What we have learned through this transformation of stale school processes into these micro-CLEs is that students and their families are able to see in action what is too often only expressed through unapplied jargon—that they have the strengths and resources among themselves to meet their own needs, meet their own challenges, and solve their own problems.

Our Family Wisdom Exchange process has been acknowledged by leaders in the school district, and their impacts have been recognized by students and their families. Over the past few years, we have consulted with our local district regarding the "parent engagement" aspects of their parent academies, contributed to the development of multi-aged mentoring programs across building levels in the district, and facilitated staff development at both building and district levels. We have engaged in this work to support the development and the educational impact of youth and their families. In doing so we work to rehabilitate how public schools view underserved communities from a lens of limitations and deficiencies to strengths and assets.

Within the University of North Florida (UNF), we have also applied the axioms, theory of change, and pedagogies of the CLE to a wide range of contexts. We have worked with academic departments to plan and facilitate developmental retreats focused on breaking through the traditional barriers of academic disciplines, and strategizing ways to embed our work more fully within the communities outside of the university. Beyond discreet academic units, we have constructed full-day, university–community exchanges around the challenges, opportunities, and value of community-based instruction within the context of university and community partnerships. Most recently, along with Matt Militello, we facilitated a Board of Trustees retreat by engaging the UNF president, trustees, provost, deans, and the rest of the university leadership team in an InQuiry process designed to render institutional strategic planning more collective, inclusive, and generative.

As our Jacksonville CLE team continues to change and grow while expanding and deepening our work to facilitate community development of hope and agency, we continue to look for ways to nurture our own development and growth within our team. We have learned from these efforts and our work together that our relationships are more generative and our work is more effective when we bring our families into the CLE work with us. This understanding began to develop more rapidly when a team member challenged us during one of our planning meetings by saying, "For all our chatter about the importance of 'inviting the stranger,' it has struck me that in our group, the stranger seems to be some of our spouses, partners, and kids."

Our planning meetings and our CLEs are now whole-family affairs. During the national CLE hosted by our Jacksonville team around the theme of "Moral Courage," participants included team members' children, spouses, parents, siblings, and cousins. This degree of family involvement has been helpful and useful in a number of ways. One of these ways is how the presence and involvement of our families signals to other participants that we are involved in this from a sense of profound moral call. It is vocation in the deep theological and ontological sense described by Frederich Buechner—vocation as the intersection between

PHOTO 4.9 Murray Hill Christ Community Church, Jacksonville, FL. Photographer: Christopher Janson.

the world's great needs and our own deepest passions. That we are not outsiders who drop in and out of communities and the issues confronting them but rather members of the community who believe in our collective capacity to address and overcome those issues enough to share in the design, development, and organization is the best way we know how to unleash that capacity.

These occasions provide great opportunities for all of the adults to involve themselves in the support and development of the children at our CLEs and our communities. Nestled in the safety and support of our CLEs, we get to see our children show great courage while learning in very public ways with and from diverse groups of those whom Horton called "extraordinary ordinary people." Our children, in turn, get to experience the impact their voices, wisdom, and experiences have on the adults in their homes, schools, and communities as well as on the issues facing them. It is our hope that by honoring our commitment to intergenerational learning, we are preparing the next generations to assume the lead in the next iterations of collective leadership for organizational and community transformation.

Reference and Further Readings

Cervantes, M. (2005). *Don Quixote* (E. Grossman, Trans.). New York, NY: Harper Perennial. (Original work published 1605–1615)

Horton, M., Freire, P., Bell, B., Gaventa, J., & Peters, J. (1990). *We make the road by walking: Conversations on education and social change.* Philadelphia, PA: Temple University Press.

Jacobs, D. (2003). *The Myles Horton reader: Education for social change.* Knoxville: University of Tennessee Press.

5

STORYMAKING

Making Sense of the Lived Experiences

Mapping the Social Experience of the Learning

The stories originating from first personal point view are critical to the development of the self. Ownership of the lived experiences and use of a specific values system create the space for teaching and learning, and building organizations and communities. The process for social engagement sets the climate and conditions for the axioms to come to life. In the opening story we see this when Miguel's curious children wanted to know "everything." The social experience was manifest as exploration, imagination, and play. This is at the core of good learning theory.

Matt's story reminds us that the celebration of life is measured in how we live it. The CLE work teaches us that when young people have good stories and thus good memories, it is typically the result of having lived good experiences. Empowering young people to be courageous and lead typically takes little more than providing them the space to do so. In a CLE, stories are shared as we create and nurture the safe spaces and healthy opportunities where participants can tell stories across generations.

The story of organizational impact presented in the assets-mapping narrative is an idea in action that begins with a belief in a value system and its accompanying theory of change. The belief leads to an invitation to develop staff, teachers, parents, students, and other stakeholders. Though personal, organizational, and community-building processes often transpire in organic ways, purposeful decision making and planning drive the work. Storytelling is part of that intentionality. Organizational and community teams that attend a CLE are prepared well before they travel to the CLE destination. Each team member is prepared with reflective questions, readings, ideas, and expectations. The excitement of traveling across the country to be with people they had never met and imagining the possibilities and opportunities outweighed the anxiety and nervous energy many of us feel. At times, teams that travel together are so immersed in conversation that they are disappointed when they are assigned different hotel rooms; participants of multiple CLEs end up requesting their same roommates so they can continue the meaningful conversations they have begun during the day. It is common to see CLE participants stay up until odd hours of the night deep in conversation.

We also see the story of change at the community level when Chris, who lives and works in Jacksonville, shares the impact his learning has had on his teaching and the way he now lives life as a public educator in his community. During CLEs in North Carolina and South Texas, Chris and his team learned about the art of hosting. Seeing friendly faces waiting at the airport when you arrive at an unknown place eases the possible stress of traveling to new communities; arriving at a different geographic and cultural place to discuss difficult issues can be a scary proposition. The social experience is at the core of an engaged pedagogy, and the invitation to dive into important conversations propels the curriculum for the CLE. The curriculum development process for the exchange is a planning and development process in itself. True to its name, the planning is collaborative, dialogical, and dynamic. We use the planning to introduce each other and the work in a way that is responsive and respectful to the local context, history, and people. The planning process begins several months in advance of the CLE event and continues through the duration of the CLE and its closing process.

Event planning is guided in formative, summative, and descriptive ways. Use of the observed and lived experience of the planning team and their networks informs the daily direction and activity. Participants are engaged and active in the assessment process, and like Dominic's story when he facilitated Circle at his grandfather's funeral, CLE participants become owners and practitioners of the pedagogies. Chris's story is similar, as he describes the impact of the CLE upon returning home to share the experiences with important people in our lives. The length of typical CLEs can vary from half a day to three days, but we also facilitate CLEs that endure for more sustained lengths of time, particularly when the topic and community require longer interventions. A weeklong CLE is not uncommon. The duration is normally negotiated with the host organization of a CLE and often depends on issues of space, resources, accessibility to site and community visits, and other logistical considerations. The local history and stories are critical to the pedagogy of a CLE. This social experience is more effective when we bring the history of the place into the conversation to inform the learning. In the history of the CLE, we have hosted gatherings in community centers, libraries, museums, beachfront hotels, ski resorts (during ski off season), Native American reservations, public parks, schools, and universities. We have also hosted CLEs in people's homes, folk and storytelling centers, local non-profit organizations, national non-profit organizations, and even on an organic farm, and in simple yet elegant and relevant public spaces like parks, nature preserves, and local lakes and rivers important to life in communities. The assets the facilitation team brings with them guide the social experience of the CLE. We bring our own values, beliefs, and experiences as parts of the pedagogy; akin to this is bringing the experience of the work we have done in our communities to share at the CLE. Sharing testimonies and success stories is important, but we want to present stories both as celebrations and opportunities for meaning making of this work. The story of asset mapping is critical, just as making sense of the public learning and the way it informs how we live life is key to the learning process. The social engagement of the CLE is the first line of learning and living in the change process of the CLE.

Cognitive Experience of the Learning

Built into the lived experience of the CLE is reflection as a strategy for meaning making and deeper understanding of the stories, practices, and strategies that emerge from conversations. The cognitive experience is critical as a scaffolding process for young and seasoned learners alike. The reflective process is an important tool we use to help participants and community partners make sense of their lived experiences throughout the CLE process. We ask participants to consider several strategies as guiding benchmarks and ask them to keep the following questions in mind:

- Why is this topic and content of the CLE important?
- What does this experience mean to me at the personal, organizational, and community levels?
- How did you use the tools and strategies presented to make sense of the engagement process?
- What can this process look like in your community?

The reflective questions help make sense of the dynamic-critical pedagogies and stories shared, created, and re-authored during a CLE. The cognitive experience gives us permission to search for change within our networks, our communities, and ourselves. We see this experience manifest when Chris returned home and shared CLE stories with his wife and family; this experience has been critical to their growth as a family and citizens within their community.

The social, cognitive, and subsequent sections are not intimately connected. Chris's story of private transformation, for example, demonstrates shifts that are social and cognitive, but the changes are also evident in his work with building a team to organize a national learning exchange they would host in Jacksonville. When the CLE came to his town, his wife and kids were in the middle of the planning, facilitating, and supporting. Through the long process of attending CLEs, hosting local ones, and organizing a national event, the social intercourse between the cognitive understanding and the personal experience elevated the awareness of the CLE work to a different depth and breadth of social, cognitive, relational, and spiritual understanding of Chris's way of life.

Discussing, Analyzing, and Critiquing Our Stories

The stories we share are not always of our own creation. We have learned them from our parents, siblings, friends, co-workers, and community members. The media adds another layer to the stories, and our educational system bombards us with stories of certainty and single truths. The CLE allows the fomenting of multiple realities, because contexts are different and stories are different, and context and story both shape realities. The process where participants share, analyze, and retell their story does not happen in a lecture format; instead, it is built into a more comfortable and inviting set of engaged strategies. We use one-on-one conversations, *pláticas*, triads, travel (as in car rides to site visits, wherein intentional conversations occur), and story mapping to enumerate select strategies. This process is where we begin to look at what is present, to examine values at work, to look at gaps in the work and in the stories, and to reflect on how stories can be reframed to yield different impacts. All must be done to engage in relevant and purposeful action.

In Matt's story, we see the awareness of youth, namely, Dominic and his younger brothers, who frame the questions about their grandfather's pictures. Their curiosity and need to know became their system of inquiry that transpired as a circle conversation in a collective and public manner. The CLE training afforded Dominic the skills to act and explore the collective story, and to invite new relationships in the room to take shape. These simple strategies can have a profound impact. The strategies are not stagnant activities, but experiences and learning theories in action that mold the rhythm of CLE. Analyses and critiques are purposeful and developmental, not attempts to stump people or to judge their values or their life experiences. The storymaker models this work as the storytelling process engages in introspection and begins to reorganize and find inspiration within his or her story.

Making meaning of the stories shared in the previous chapter and stories we share in daily life can be difficult to the untrained eye. As story is employed as a key educational tool in the transmission of values, culture, and community building through the work of the CLE, we make sense of the concept of story through a disciplined approach. The rhythm employed at the CLE of telling a story, critically analyzing the story, and using the lessons learned to inform the next community action helps inform the lessons and organization of this chapter. The previous chapter highlights the storytelling process in public and is organized by the rhythm of ecologies of knowing. Though the stories have their stand alone and contextual meaning, an analysis for deeper meaning making requires deliberate guidance so the learning can be accessible to the ears, eyes, hands, legs, and heart of the participant. We propose a tool for meaning making that guides analysis and understanding of the stories we share. This tool is an invitation to scaffold the lessons from stories through the use of a matrix that guides the mapping of the stories in the previous chapter. Embedded in the matrix are the ecologies of knowing as the foundational organizing tool. Axioms are laid over to present a two-dimensional landscape for placement of the different lived experiences in the stories. This multi-layered framework is then transferred into a matrix for utility. This exercise is neither to judge the stories nor to essentialize them, because to do so would kill the spirit of what we believe and practice story to be as a core pedagogy of the CLE. The goal is to share CLE strategies to help the reader make meaning of the story during the critique phase of the engagement process. This process helps place story with the axioms and ecologies as we help each other better understand the stories, the people, their history, and passions. The purpose of this process is relationship building that will help facilitate and navigate meaningful engagement. We provide a matrix of the axioms and ecologies below. It is placed here for the reader to think about how stories are situated among the axioms and ecologies.

The stories are narratives of action, as acting and enacting are cornerstones of the CLE work. Stories provide an opportunity where CLE participants serve as witnesses to their public life. The stories of self, organizations, and communities

Intersections of Ecologies and Axioms in Lived Experiences

	Ecologies		
Axioms	*Self*	*Organization*	*Community*
Learning and leadership are a dynamic social process			
Conversations are critical and central pedagogical processes			
The people closest to the issues are best situated to discover answers to local concerns			
Crossing boundaries enriches the development and educational process			
Hope and change are built on assets and dreams of locals and their communities			

are manifest as a public pedagogy and a journey of exploration. And the stories interface with the ecologies, as the narratives Miguel and Matt tell were shaped by CLE experiences that nurtured the self. The Llano Grande story describes the organization guided by its faith in families, in youth, and in community. The importance of Llano Grande's work is marked by the stories of youth building a local organization, building the local community, and working to build a local economy through their steadfast belief in their community cultural wealth. The stories present examples of how local people act through their stories; it is also a way they "give legs" to their stories they experience. The actions taken in Chris's community in north Florida capture the multiple ecologies of knowing: self, organization, and community. Individuals were changed as they thought about their lives in critically self reflective ways; organizations looked inward differently, as they thought about the relationships they built with other organizations across the region; and communities at large were challenged to think about history in different ways. The interaction between the three levels played itself out through the planning for the national event, and in its internal evaluative report, the Jacksonville team felt it had turned a corner in terms of knowing how to deal with issues of racial justice and healing. The CLE became the place through which the transformation was realized. Mobility and flexibility are frames built into the CLE curriculum. The curriculum is dynamic and the meaning-making process flexible, and both are essential conditions that allow stories to be acted out. As we re-author ourselves, we change our organizations and transform our communities. If the conditions continue to be nurtured, the process of healthy change can be sustained.

Re-Authoring Our Stories, Conditions, and Actions

The idea of a blank canvas is a useful symbol to help make sense of the developmental quality of CLE work. Because all participants bring wisdom to the CLE, we use this visual as an example of the collective actions of those involved in a learning exchange.

A blank canvas was presented to more than 80 participants at the beginning of a CLE. The adjoining canvas is the collective artistic contribution of individual CLE team participants, a simple yet tangible example of the re-authoring process of a collective awareness. The engagement processes challenge us to think about our story and to re-author it with others. The scope, values, and delivery of the story is up to each of us, but the context for engagement, experiences, opportunities for conversations, and invitation to reimagine the core of who we are—the work we do and how we do it—is the function of the Community Learning Exchange. The ability to re-author the self includes the willingness to ask questions of those around us in a reflective and comparative way. The process of re-authoring is grounded in the ontology of courage and the willingness

PHOTO 5.1 Jacksonville CLE finished portrait. Photographer: Matthew Militello.

to change the context and conditions in which we live our lives. The action of change at the CLE is inviting your gifts and asking every participant: What is your story? The opportunity to re-author ourselves is the most radical work we do. When participants move themselves to a collective space, they realize the power of change. Re-authoring the self can be self-evident while at a CLE, but the acting on our newly developed awareness of self, organization, and community requires us to be active about our learning as we employ the CLE pedagogies in public spaces and in public ways.

Closing the Circle

In the aftermath of the Jacksonville CLE participants reflected through the use of Circle. Numerous participants said the gift the CLE afforded them was the invitation to engage in conversation, reflect in a public space, and re-author themselves as public people. These are the stories of action experienced when the conditions, support, skills, and imagination converge with the right level of tension. Our commitment is to move each other to this stage. To scaffold this action within this text, we provide the ontology of an idea, examples of the work, and stories that chronicle the impact of the work at multiple levels. To live this vicariously does not have the same effect on our awareness as when we are present. We invite you to explore the possibilities of bringing this idea to life as you work to identify issues in your life that move you to action. We hope you make meaning of this multi-layered socially constructed body of work that is personal at the core, public in practice, and radical in participation. This politic is what brings spirit to our lives as parents, siblings, friends, and public educators. Making meaning of this work will help you and your team, organization, school, or community find the appropriate moral and political compass to inform your next public education action.

Your role is to learn the rhythm of the process and build the skills and the relationships necessary to invite others as you develop a collective critical consciousness that surfaces when we *unite the power of place and wisdom of people.* The balance of these forces within the local ecologies makes the lived experiences transformational. We invite you to explore the mapping of stories by using the matrix in this chapter. This practice will help you understand the context, the people, their stories, their dreams, and their actions. If you find this tool for mapping the stories helpful, we are certain you will find the next chapters in this book useful also. In Part III, we present a more complete presentation of the CLE pedagogies. We have created, borrowed, and taught these dynamic-critical pedagogies to help CLE participants and communities transform themselves, their organizations, and communities. We believe that these pedagogies will also transform your work as learners, teachers, and leaders.

PART III
Dynamic-Critical Pedagogies

DRAWING 3 Artwork by Mónica Valadez.

Source: Mónica Valadez. Used with permission.

6

TEACHING FOR LEARNING, LEARNING TO TEACH

So many local people hold the stories and wisdom needed to uncover historical truths and the agency to generate a way forward. Meaningful interventions and sustained practice are grounded in local people and the values they hold. Nevertheless, communities need the capacity to build skills to understand and infuse these values. This chapter highlights ways to engage communities in this work. We struggled to name these. Are they strategies, methods, designs, social technologies, or procedures? In the end, we kept coming back to dynamic-critical pedagogies—*where knowledge and action are co-constructed by teachers, learners, and community partners.* Teaching alone does not capture the interactive nature of the Community Learning Exchange work. Dynamic-critical pedagogy is a process that includes teaching and learning, action and inquiry, knowledge and reflection, skills and generosity to engage and honor people.

The pedagogies are adaptable to a variety of environments and depend on context. Community members should be consulted *prior to* the enactment of any strategy. The CLE teaches us that when the pedagogies are used together, greater community change can occur, rather than when communities become overly dependent on only one pedagogy. The pedagogies should be used based on the unique strengths and needs of each community.

Understanding Learning to Be a Teacher

For us, learning is a result of teaching that is engaging, empowering, challenging, inspiring, and applicable. That is, learning must transform from *data* (raw and unfiltered) to *information* (filtered data through some mediating source, e.g., a teacher or the media), then to *knowledge* (contextualized information), and finally to *application* (knowledge to action). The real test of learning resides in the application.

Our knowledge is latent—merely potential until circumstance and conditions are conducive for development. Once activated, the knowledge becomes kinetic; this kinetic knowledge must be fortified with information that informs action that must be factual, thorough, and thoughtful. CLE practices and pedagogies are catalysts that allow this shift to occur.

Teaching and learning do not occur in a vacuum. There is a context to life in and out of schools for children, and in and out of various organizational and institutional structures and cultures for adults. The learner's past experience, personal interests, and prior knowledge must be understood for information to be transformed into knowledge. As a result, the contexts of the individual meaning making are crafted, reinforced, and mitigated by internal and external forces, especially the contexts of place and culture.

We also hold the strong belief that teaching in this manner must be reciprocal. Teaching and learning are interdependent—the title or position of teacher and learner does not regulate one as the knowledge dispenser and the other as an empty receptacle to be filled. Rather, the interdependency is a principle of learning reciprocity whereby interaction around information, theory, and action spawns new learning from everyone. When, and only when, teaching and learning are interdependent will there be meaning making from knowledge and subsequently application (action). Inherent in this process is a vulnerability from participants. This allows a sharing of power, a democratization of learning. This interdependency and vulnerability, coupled with the CLE axioms and RASPPA, lead to the gold standard of teaching and learning: action *and* inquiry. *Action needs inquiry, and inquiry needs action.* Any imbalance can lead to action before thinking, on one hand and never acting and only questioning, on the other.

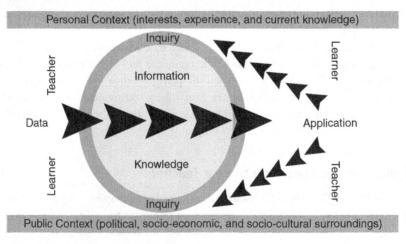

FIGURE 6.1 Teaching and learning and inquiry and action

There is an old adage that teachers are like comedians. This may be true in the entertainment sense, but there is a deeper message of learning in this comparison. The success of a joke resides in the ability of the audience to *get it*. Jokes are funny not only for the sarcasm or wit but because the audience has an immediate reaction predicated on understanding. If a member of the audience has to say "I don't get it," then the joke loses all potency. Sure, the comedian can restate the joke with more context and explanation, but the laughter that follows is usually muffled at best—thus the adage that says you cannot rehabilitate a joke.

Every day, teachers are entrusted to help students (children, adolescents, and adult learners) *get it*. When students don't get it, there is a missed opportunity for learning that may never be the same. As a result, what they already know about students, empathy for one's own learning process, and how they choose to teach (pedagogical strategies) becomes vitally important in the transformation of information into knowledge.

The CLE Pedagogies for Engagement and Learning

The dynamic-critical pedagogies that we have employed in our work have been tested—they are not tried and true but tested. In fact, the pedagogies are filled with stories of success and failure, with engagement and laughter, and with tension and tears. The pedagogies are gifts brought by CLE organizers and participants. Thus, we are continually adding pedagogies to our repertoire. The pedagogies are evolving and fluid. We use feedback and reflection as well as the invitation to have participants re-author the strategies we employ. The CLE pedagogies are in a constant state of change. The pedagogies are relevant, provocative, malleable, and emanate from the CLE axioms lived in RASPPA. Most importantly, they are continuously practiced.

Throughout the book, we name a number of these pedagogies in action. We highlight some of the impacts the pedagogies have had and continue to have on those who engage in this work. Following is a set of CLE pedagogies that we use in our work—in CLEs as well as our work in our professions, communities, and homes.

The art and theory of CLE pedagogies is grounded in the idea that people's stories and actions are bridged through mediating factors we call pedagogies. CLE participants learn these skills, strategies, and processes through relationships and conversations. Individuals and groups are offered a space and place to imagine, plan for action, build new relationships, renew their call, and learn strategies to liberate their practice when they return to their communities.

Reflections on CLE Pedagogies

We seek to honor the work of others and our elders as we try to press these pedagogies into the mainstream of work for self, organization, and community.

We see these pedagogies as strategies rooted in history and culture. These pedagogies are not bound by what is written. That is, there is no right way, no one metric or rubric—there are no singular tonics that lead to and measure success. Rather, we offer these ways of learning in collaboration (relationships) and context (place)—always situated in Gracious Space. These pedagogies are ways to solicit and elicit in an organic, invitational manner.

We know this work to be life changing and radical in many settings. The pedagogies are liberating forces that allow for rehabilitating ancient, effective practices as well as the construction of new strategies of engaged, dynamic learning. In our experience, these pedagogies are

- *Invitational:* Where all are welcome, locals and outsiders, elders and the young, known members and strangers
- *Empowering:* Where people who may have previously been silenced or marginalized have a substantial voice
- *Relational:* Where stories are told, honored, and heard
- *Engaging:* Where people share their wisdom with known and new networks to unpack and address difficult issues
- *Experiential:* Where real work is tried in a real setting, with participants providing the case study rather than exploring outside case studies
- *Impacting:* Where action plans are designed and executed to develop new narratives for healing
- *Public:* Where people are free to operate in community spaces free of judgment
- *Reflective:* Where time and space are carved out for individual and group analysis
- *Rejuvenating:* Where the spirit is restored and new dreams are advanced

★ ★ ★ ★ ★ ★

These dynamic-critical pedagogies have allowed us to mediate the intersections of theory and practice, people and place, and spirit and humanity. This is the work of the CLE. In the next two chapters we highlight these pedagogies that we have used at various national and local Community Learning Exchanges. We have divided these pedagogies into two categories: (a) dynamic-critical pedagogies of reflection and (b) dynamic-critical pedagogies with and in community.

These dynamic-critical pedagogies are not rigid or static; they are fluid and dynamic. Our desire is to give enough guidance and examples of practices for the reader. We therefore encourage you to modify the pedagogies or even create and share your own strategies. Our hope is that these pedagogies meet the needs of multiple teaching and learning styles and provide you with the license to make the pedagogies meaningful in your own work.

References and Further Readings

Dewey, J. (1963). *Experience and education*. New York, NY: Collier Books.

Freire, P. (1997). *Pedagogy of the oppressed*. New York, NY: Continuum.

Hughes, P., & Grace, B. (2010). *Gracious Space: A practical guide to working together* (2nd ed.). Seattle, WA: Center for Ethical Leadership.

Militello, M., Rallis, S.F., & Goldring, E.B. (2009). *Leading with inquiry and action: How principals improve teaching and learning*. Thousand Oaks, CA: Corwin Press.

Petrides, L.A., & Guiney, S.Z. (2002). Knowledge management for school leaders: An ecological framework for thinking schools. *Teachers College Record, 104*(8), 1702–1717.

Rawls, J. (1971). *A theory of justice*. Cambridge, MA: Harvard University Press.

7

DYNAMIC-CRITICAL PEDAGOGIES OF REFLECTION

We believe in the importance of reflection and practice it with great diligence. Individual and group reflection is usually relegated to the end of a process or event, if it is intentionally placed on the agenda at all. Too often this step is passed over when we are running short of time. Reflection must be intentional and it must be understood as not only a summative or evaluative strategy, but also a critical element of understanding, listening, and learning. Reflection should not be a simple "reporting out." Reflective practices pave the way for change—individually and organizationally. Dynamic reflection—thinking and talking alone and with others—creates a situation where current knowledge, skills, and practices are unpacked and modified, if needed.

This chapter highlights a set of "pedagogies of reflection," specific strategies to engage in thinking, listening, and dialogue for learning. Each of the pedagogies is designed for immediate implementation. However, each honors your own expertise, interpretation, context, and needs. After each of the pedagogies is described, we provide an example of the pedagogy in action—an account of the use in a national or local CLE. Finally, we highlight links to videos for you to *see* the pedagogy in action. The video links can be found in *Video Links* categorized by the specific pedagogies.

CIRCLE

Circle draws on longtime rituals of cultures and communities that provide space to open up fresh possibilities for connections, collaboration, and understanding. Circle can hold the tensions and emotions that contribute to healing and can support people to use collective energy to take action. The process is not about changing others but acts as an invitation to change one's relationship with oneself, to one's organization, and to the wider community. The result is the development of strong relationships, trust, and the ability to work together to advance social justice in communities.

Circle taps into ancient practices and modern processes to create trust, goodwill, belonging, and reciprocity. It offers a way of being together that transforms relationships. Participants sit in a circle, and in the center is a collection of symbolic objects placed to remind participants of values shared among those in the Circle. A talking piece is used as a way to ensure respect between speakers and listeners. The talking piece is passed from person to person within the Circle, and only the person holding the piece may speak. The talking piece holds great symbolic importance, and warrants explanation of its selection by the Circle convener. Talking pieces have also been used in different ways. For instance, instead of one talking piece, Circle participants have been asked to bring their own talking pieces. Each participant describes the piece and offers it to the center of the Circle. In the end, there is representation of objects that can then be discussed. Along with the importance of the process and the design of the Circle, the development of the prompt for each Circle must be purposeful and authentic—attending to the organic nature of the CLE.

Theoretical Underpinnings

Circle builds community by ensuring that each person has an equal voice. Circle democratizes discourse in ways first imaged by indigenous communities. Circle brings people together in healthy ways. They can build new relationships, strengthen old ones, and restore those relationship that have been damaged. Circles:

- **Create safety and trust.** Mistrust can be a logical survival strategy for people who have been unfairly treated by others. Creating safe space can allow trust to develop in a natural way.
- **Honor voice and hold stories sacred.** To tap the wisdom people hold, we need to hear their stories. When we treat these stories in a sacred manner, people will be more inclined to share what is most important to them.
- **Share power among people.** When people come together, there is often a significant difference in the power they carry, particularly when a participant has a formal position of leadership in the community or in an organization. Power needs to be held lightly so the value of each person can surface. We need to affirm the dignity of everyone based on his or her humanity and not the person's title.
- **Support honest dialogue about important issues.** We need people to be able to talk about the most important issues facing the community. This requires moving past reluctance and opening up to honest dialogue.
- **Foster new relationships.** Sometimes groups will open up honest comments about issues and fail to work through the pain and dissonance that emerges. Community gatherings can work through difficult discomfort and pain in a way that builds stronger, deeper connections and relationships among people.

Outcome

The outcomes of Circle include democratizing voice, bringing reflection into the public sphere, and eliciting and honoring collective wisdom.

Application

Circle can be used in numerous scenarios and for many purposes. It is well established as a model for opening up deeper relationships and honest conversations in organizations. The Circle process has been used to foster understanding between nurse practitioners and teenage parents; to bring together faculty from an academic program at a regional state university; and to connect students, school board members, parents, and teachers to improve local schools. Circle has also been used to address inter-generational work, racism, violence, and police–community relationships as well as to provide alternatives within the justice system.

CLE Implementation

In Community Learning Exchanges, we routinely use Circle as a way to open and close the gatherings. We use it to go deeper into issues when it is important to hear all voices and perspectives to create collective understanding of issues. Following are the steps that a Circle keeper should follow when conducting a Circle.

Process for Opening Circle

- Gather in a circle, making sure everyone can be seen by one another.
- Use a talking piece that is meaningful to the purpose of the gathering.
- Welcome people and offer a reading, poem, quote, or story to set the tone and bring good spirit into the gathering.
- Invite people to introduce themselves, say where they are from, and answer a prompt around one of the following:
  - o reflections about the personal gifts they are bringing to the CLE.
  - o reflections around ways they hope they change from the CLE.
  - o stories around the theme or topic of the CLE.
  - o invocations of others in their lives who support their courage to change and grow during CLE.
- Introduce the talking piece and explain ground rules for its movement around the Circle: Only the person with the talking piece speaks; each speaker passes the talking piece to the left. As the talking piece goes from person to person, each is asked to respond to the prompt, and the talking piece is passed to the next person after each response. Each person with the talking piece is

encouraged to speak from the heart, and the other participants are encouraged to listen with an open heart and to hold back comments on what others say.

Process for Closing Circle

- Remind participants of the role and significance of the talking piece.
- Introduce the closing reflection prompt around one of the following:
  - o reflections around what has moved you during our time together.
  - o ways that they believe they have changed as a result of the CLE.
  - o new hopes resulting from emergent understandings or stories around them or topic of the CLE.
  - o appreciations for the others at the CLE who supported their growth and development.
  - o invitations to share plans of action upon their return home.
- The size of Circle may dictate a time limit for each participant's Circle story. Invite one person to do final closing reflection about this gathering (arrange this prior to starting the closing of Circle).

Circle in Action

This work has been shaped by the innovative work of the Center for Ethical Leadership (see *Web Links*). CEL uses healing circles in communities across the world. In Community Learning Exchanges (CLE), we most frequently employ Circle as a way to *open and close* gatherings and to debrief site visits. As an opening, we use Circle to (a) set the tone for the topic of the convening, (b) introduce participants of the convening, and (c) provide a background for the setting/place where the convening is being held. In site visits, we use Circle to reflect on thoughts and emotions participants experience from being in a particular place. As a closing, we employ Circle (a) to share new lessons learned and (b) to announce future actions and practices.

CLE Circle Examples

Educators and community members from across the country use Circle to help understand what *Collective Leadership* is and what it looks like. A short clip of that discussion can be found in the *Video Links*.

In North Carolina, participants gathered in Circle to open the CLE. Before the individual introductions were made, local experts provided a short history of the place. The North Carolina gathering was held at a former slave plantation (see *Video Links*). Participants heard the history of the *place*, offered public acknowledgments to ancestors who experienced slavery, and followed with a ceremonial ringing of a bell chimed for each ancestor.

Opening Circles have also deviated from the tradition of each participant addressing the opening question. In Washington, DC, two Circles were created, one with youth and one with elders. Each Circle discussed expectations while the other group listened. Afterward, smaller Circles of youth and elders were created to have deeper discussions about the perspectives of youth and elders.

Opening Circles have also been used to introduce teams rather than individuals. Prior to a convening in Seattle, Washington, teams were asked to bring an artifact that represented their team or their work together. Together the team used the artifact to introduce who they were and the work they were passionate about.

During closing Circle in North Carolina, the talking piece that was chosen was a branch from the surrounding cotton fields. This branch became a powerful, emotional artifact of the work that was taken on by the teams. The branch was symbolic of both the past and the future. The closing Circle was enriched by the thoughtful consideration of the talking piece.

APPRECIATIVE LISTENING PROTOCOL

The purpose of the appreciative listening protocol is to share with a partner a story that connects you personally to the learning. Sometimes listening or silence is difficult with persons new to the protocol. At times, the listener wants to ask questions, but the listener should refrain from this to help the speaker reflect and construct his or her thinking. Even if there is silent time, it is useful for the speaker's thinking. The work of Julian Weissglass and Lynda Tredway have been influential to this protocol.

Norms for Engagement

- Assume best intentions.
- Listen fully to a partner, sitting eye-to-eye and knee-to-knee (as is culturally appropriate).
- If there is silence in the designated talk time for one person, that is fine.
- As the listener, do not comment, give feedback, or add your story. You are listening, not editing, and giving your fullest attention to the speaker. The listener may use nonverbal responses.
- Maintain double confidentiality. You will not repeat a story heard, and you will not ask your partner about the story he or she tells outside of this exercise unless he or she raises it again with you.

Facilitator Role

You may want to model this with a willing person if this is the first time you are using appreciative or constructive listening with a group. Introduce it as a way to have someone listen to you completely without judgment for a designated time (usually two minutes). Start with dyads (twos/duets).

- A facilitator reviews directions and keeps time.
- State norms of engagement. Ask if there are questions.
- Prepare and have participants respond to a designated prompt.

- Let everyone get settled with a partner. If they do not know each other (or know each other well), give them time for interchange before starting. Have the dyad decide who goes first. Be a "warm demander" on the protocols for the dyad, as it is uncomfortable for some at first—but necessary.
- The first person shares for two minutes (or a determined time) *without interruption*, even if he or she is silent. The listener may give nonverbal feedback or sub-vocalization like "umm" but does not include verbal feedback, questions, other stories, and so on.
- Facilitator joins the single person if there is an uneven number.
- Provide clear "bordering" of this activity by keeping time and saying "go" and "stop" after two minutes. Make sure the dyads change partners.
- Debrief the activity at the end, accept all responses, but do not defend the process. It takes some people longer to get used to this than others.
- Two minutes for cross-sharing may be added to the end of the protocol.
- Remind participants of double confidentiality at the end of the process.

Adaptations

- You may decide to do this in trios after your community has done the dyad work frequently, but do not recommend starting with this.
- You can choose to have full discussion after, but remember norms. Depending on the content being shared, you may choose to ask participants to contribute their ideas—but not their partners'—to maintain double confidentiality.

Appreciative Listening in Action

In Community Learning Exchanges, we have used appreciative listening to (a) create spaces for discussing difficult topics and (b) allow for deep interactions with individuals who did not previously know one another.

Appreciative Listening Examples

In Washington, DC, appreciative listening was used around the topic of advocacy. In pairs, participants took turns discussing a time when they had to advocate for themselves. Following the protocol, pairs were able to deeply listen to one another and then reflect on what they heard.

UNPLANNED BUT INTENTIONAL ENGAGEMENT

We believe learning occurs when conversation is present. Conversations at CLEs happen in planned and unplanned settings. It is important to consider every interaction to be an opportunity to be intentional about conversations and sharing. As we have shared there is power in story and in people sharing and hearing one another's stories. While sharing stories can be encouraged through pedagogies such as the Journey Line, we have found that people naturally begin to find other people to connect to at CLEs. These connections happen in many ways, for many reasons. We have seen that some of the most meaningful connections occur when people reach beyond easy, and comfortable affinities and seek connection with those who they believe they might best learn from in the moment, or around the topic or concern they are experiencing.

Unplanned, Intentional Engagement in Action

We wanted to call this the "pedagogy of the van" after discovering powerful conversations were taking place while participants were traveling to and from locations during the CLE. Participants are encouraged to be purposeful about who they sit next to in order to engage in further conversations. We recognized the pedagogical possibilities of times and spaces often ignored transition times.

Unplanned, Intentional Engagement Examples

We encourage participants to reach out to individuals or teams to initiate conversations. For instance, we have asked participants to reach out to specific individuals. While traveling by vans to site visit locations during the Jacksonville CLE, participants were invited to pair up with those from other communities in order to share local stories of moral courage. While initial prompts are provided and suggested, these conversations are not scripted, but rather move to they rhythm of the needs of the conversation partners or groups.

MEANINGFUL CONVERSATIONS

Meaningful conversation is the heartbeat of any learning exchange, what follows here is a generic pedagogy. The essential parts of a conversation are the relationship(s) between or among the participants and the important moments in a conversation that stimulate the persons participating in the conversation to reflect and act. All conversation is narrative, and through the narrative, we can develop and exercise agency. The work of Lynda Tredway has been influential to the CLE adaptation of this pedagogy.

Theoretical Underpinnings

Pláticas are an expressive cultural form shaped by listening, inquiring, storytelling, and storymaking that is akin to a nuanced, multi-dimensional conversation. These conversations are told in native languages and with culturally relevant traditions. *Pláticas* are meaningful conversations.

Outcomes

There are two outcomes of the Meaningful Conversations pedagogy: (a) to identify and discuss examples of structured and less structured conversations that occur in the CLE context and (b) to analyze components of Meaningful Conversations.

Application and Implementation

The Meaningful Conversation that leads to collective sense making is a part of all Community Learning Exchange pedagogies (Circle, World Café, InQuiry, etc.). Multiple protocols and processes can contribute to the conversations.

Following is an example of activities and timing that could comprise a short CLE session on the importance of Meaningful Conversation:

Time	Question or Activity	Process
8 min	What is one meaningful conversation you have had in your work experience?	Appreciative listening protocol
8 min	How would you analyze that conversation in terms of the framework below?	See ranges below
8 min	How does conversation represent a story about you, a group, or a time of action/advocacy?	Analyzing conversation
6 min	Questions and debriefing	

Range of Experience and Engagement for Meaningful Conversations

More structured_____	Less structured
Deeply engaging_____	Less engaging
Public_____	Private
Personal_____	Political
Arranged_____	By choice

Meaningful Conversations in Action

At a Community Learning Exchange, Meaningful Conversations are the intent of everything that is done. Through conversations, there will be shared understandings, new meaning-making, and a networked call to action. As such, we are purposeful regarding Meaningful Conversations.

Meaningful Conversations Examples

At a CLE held at the Highlander Center in New Market, Tennessee, participants engaged in Meaningful Conversations throughout the CLE about pre-K through post-secondary education. Toward the end of the CLE, we asked a number of participants to summarize their conversations about education—in order to shape a new educational narrative (See *Video Links* for a short video).

INQUIRY

Q methodology is a culturally relevant way to engage communities in data collection and dialogue. It was initially developed in the 1950s as a way of understanding the attitudes and values that individuals hold toward a particular issue or topic. Q methodology uses distinct psychometric principles and operational procedures in order to provide researchers with the means to systematically and rigorously identify, describe, and examine human subjectivity.

Q methodology is a powerful tool to help understand people's values, attitudes, and perspectives. The method allows evaluators to maintain a very close proximity to participant subjectivity, a proximity that is believed to honor and maintain the integrity of participants' cultural identities. In fact, Q methodology has been called a "methodology for the marginalized." We have found the methodology especially useful in historically marginalized communities where there is a reluctance to engage in traditional evaluative processes.

Theoretical Underpinnings

Q methodology is a tool that uniquely bridges qualitative and quantitative data in a single analytic lens. The subjectivity (i.e., individual ideas) that participants express is collected from the individual responses they make to statements related to their attitudes about a particular topic. The way they sort the information is then translated into aggregate data for use in dialogue about the topic.

Note that some of the specifics of the evaluation process discussed in the following sections are a part of the statistical analysis the facilitators use to report the information to the group. These statistical processes and language do not need to be understood by all in order for the sort and process to work effectively.

Outcome

The outcome of InQuiry is to analyze attitudes and values about a topic by gathering a collective range of perspectives on the topic.

General Process

In specific terms, participants sort a set of statements (or other items) about a given topic in ways that reflect the complexities and nuances of their perspectives. These individual "sorts" are then subjected to statistical analyses, a factor analysis where participants, not survey items, serve as the variables. Factor analysis then yields groups of participants who cluster (factor in affinity groups) around the topic.

While this is a way to quantitatively measure and examine people's shared perspectives, the real force behind the methodology lies in the participatory nature of the process. Q methodology is highly participatory as a research approach because participants define, decide, and make meaning throughout the process. Through our CLE work, we have stretched to the traditional use of Q Methodology, extending its participatory nature much more comprehensively. Specifically, in addition to using Q Methodology to involve participants in both the construction of the data collection instrument and data collection itself, through a process we've named InQuiry, we actively engage participants in a process of collective analysis of the data (see *Web Links* for Q methodology resources and *Video Links* for a video on the InQuiry process).

Specifics of InQuiry

Arguably, no single evaluation tool or metric offers a complete understanding or validation of impact, nor does it measure the extent or depth of change as a result of a given project. However, InQuiry has a number of benefits that far outweigh its shortcomings:

- It provides insight into respondents' viewpoints related to specific issues or ideas.
- It enables sensitive issues to be explored in a way that is more directed by group perspectives (as opposed to the perspectives of the evaluator or implementer).
- It is participatory and engaging, and thus distinct from a self- or enumerator-administered survey.
- It yields statistically valid results related to the factors or clusters of items, which allows for comparison of how treatment and comparison groups might (or might not) differ in the way they perceive particular issues.

By being inclusive and participatory in its methodology, the InQuiry process matches our commitment to conducting assessments and evaluations that are participatory and enable collective engagement among participants. We have found that the participants who have responded with the most enthusiasm to being involved with this InQuiry process have most often been those representing indigenous and native communities. This is because the InQuiry process deeply honors their subjectivity—both their idiosyncratic subjectivity as individuals and their collective subjectivity of their communities found in the cultural meanings, values, understandings, and nuances that make their cultural views rich and strong. In addition, our application of Q methodology in the InQuiry process is a unique and powerful way to reduce the distinctions between evaluator and evaluated in order to collectively produce, analyze, and extend meaning from data that are at a generous proximity to participant voice. As such, this work is significant not only because it has elevated and magnified the voices of a diverse set of community members and leaders but also because InQuiry frames a process in which their voices can be applied to any given topic.

Step-by-Step Process

1. **Topic to examine subjectivity:** Name the communication topic that you want to understand. Subjectivity is communication that is self-referent; particular to a given person's point of view; existing only within the mind of the one who experiences the phenomena.
2. **Concourse:** A concourse is a collection of statements that represent the discussion about a particular topic in participants' own words and language. Note that this can include artwork, objects, behaviors, photographs, traits, cartoons, and other items.
3. **Q-set:** Also called Q-sample, a Q-set is a representative sample of items taken from the concourse that reflects the nature of the larger set of statements or representations and usually falls within a range of 18–50.
4. **Q-sort:** A Q-sort is a forced distribution ranking or scoring of items in the Q-set by participants; statements are quantified by ranking them "relative to one another." The sorts can be done either online (see links in resources) or in person using printed cards. The forced distribution can take many forms and usually looks like an upside down normal distribution.
5. **P-sample**. Individuals who perform Q-Sorts are called the P-sample (Person-sample) or P-set. The P-sample may be conveniently or theoretically structured.
6. **Statistical analysis:** PQ method (see link in resources) is the most convenient way to analyze the data. The programs allow you to enter the data and then factor analyze the data in order to create groups or families of individuals who have sorted in a similar fashion.
7. **Family analysis.** The factors derived from the statistical analysis (no. 6) can be called "families," or affinity groups or teams. In the family analysis, the affinity groups/families/teams are taken through a protocol that guides a conversation about who is at the table, the shared perspective of the sort, and how the process can impact future work. Families are asked to create a logo or theme that can be illustrated or represented on a real T-shirt or poster to highlight their learning.

Tasks of InQuiry

- **Task 1:** Determine some things group members have in common that might have led to sharing a common perspective.
- **Task 2:** Interpret your shared perspectives.
  - o The positions of these statements and their relationships with one another are the basis for interpretation.
  - o What priorities are most important to this perspective?

- **Task 3:** Name your perspective.
  - o Based on the most important priorities above, what theme emerges?
  - o If you were to create a marketing slogan from this perspective, what would it be?
  - o If this perspective were a novel, what would the title be?
- **Task 4:** Have conversations about your perspectives and implications.
  - o What are the implications of the priorities for the shared perspective(s)?
  - o What are the key strengths and advantages of these perspective(s)?
  - o What are some limitations or vulnerabilities inherent in these perspective(s)?

In Chapter 9 we provide more details about the use of InQuiry at CLEs, photos of InQuiry in action, and an example of an affinity group/family t-shirt that was created.

InQuiry in Action

In Community Learning Exchanges (CLE), we have used the InQuiry process on a number of occasions. InQuiry allows participants to deeply engage in deliberations about their beliefs around a topic. In turn, making these beliefs public has caused new, transparent understandings among participants in teams who have attended CLEs. See *Video Links* for a series of InQuiry videos.

InQuiry Examples

Developing statements for participants to sort must be an organic, inclusive process. For the CLE in Hawaii, we needed to honor the importance of family that is rooted in community work. In order to help community teams expand their work, we used the InQuiry process to first help team members understand the roles they play in their own families. Prior to the CLE, 43 statements were developed with participants:

- Wise counselor: "I advise my family with my perspective that has been informed by experiences they may not yet have encountered."
- Historian: "I am a family historian and memory keeper. I have been involved in the documentation of story from elders."
- Peacekeeper: "I promote peace and understanding between family members. This sometimes involves conflict mediation when necessary."

These deep conversations about family roles made subsequent discussions about roles people held in their home organizations more potent.

To prepare for the Montana CLE, we used an important, popular children's story from the local Native American culture. After receiving permission to use the story by tribal elders, we asked local residents to read the story on camera. This video represents a collaborative reading of *The Gift of the Bitterroot: A Salish and Pend d'Oreille Story* by Johnny Arlee and illustrated by Antoine Sandoval, and read by a number of leaders within the Confederated Salish and Kootenai Tribes and Salish Kootenai College. By serving as an allegory, *The Gift of the Bitterroot* was used here as a pedagogical and developmental instrument for the theme of the Montana CLE: "Transforming Education From an Instrument of Historical Trauma to an Instrument of Healing."

We sent the video to national experts of tribal education and to individuals who would be attending the CLE. We asked viewers to briefly describe some ways that *The Gift of the Bitterroot* could represent the story of the educational experiences of Native Americans (or other marginalized groups) in this country (see *Video Links*).

Sharing the team/family perspectices is an important part of the InQuiry process. In this video, family members at the Seattle CLE use posters to present their "Family Name" (see *Video Links*).

JOURNEY LINE

As with many of the pedagogies of the Community Learning Exchange, the Journey Line is designed to help participants tell their stories. Stories are a moving force for change. The Journey Line pedagogy provides individuals with time to create a short visual representation that helps them tell a story around a given topic.

At the Youth Advocacy CLE in Washington, DC, we challenged participants with the following Journey Line exercise:

- Think about the times in your life, from birth to your mid-20s, when you used your voice to advocate for yourself or others. These times on your personal "journey line" when you advocated for yourself or others could have been those occasions when you took on more responsibility for your own life (e.g., traveling, daily management), and/or times when you exercised formal or informal leadership of friends, activities, or organizations.
- Think about three to four of those key experiences and put them on the Journey Line below. You can indicate whether they were very important or of medium importance.

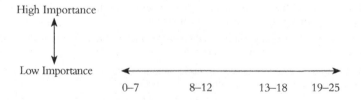

- Choose one story from your Journey Line and write or record a longer story from it.
- After reviewing the story, think about one sentence that captures your story and journey: I am the story of _____.

Both the Journey Line and the specific stories can be shared in a variety of ways. Journey Lines can be hung up and stories can be shared with others vis-à-vis a number of the pedagogies described in this book, including Appreciative Listening, Learning Walks, and Meaningful Conversations, to name a few.

Journey Line in Action

In Community Learning Exchanges, we have used the Journey Line to (a) create spaces to uncover personal experiences with difficult topics and (b) allow for deep interactions with individuals who did not previously know one another.

Journey Line Examples

At the Youth Advocacy CLE in Washington, DC, we asked participants:

Think about the times in your life, from birth to your mid-20s, when you used your voice to advocate for yourself or others, and made choices for yourself. These times on your personal "journey line" when you advocated for yourself or others could have been those occasions when you took on more responsibility for your own life (e.g., traveling, daily management), and/or times when you exercised formal or informal leadership of friends, activities, or organizations.

Here is an example of a participant's Journey Line story:

In 7th grade English class, the teacher accused my friend Anne of cheating. She called her out in front of the entire class. I was outraged because I knew Anne would never do that, and particularly no one would do it from Ronnie's paper! She was hurt and scared. I was angry. I usually went home on the school bus, but I called my mother and I said that I had to stay at school and talk to Miss Otto, the principal, because Anne needed me to. So I went to the principal's office and I explained what had happened to Miss Otto. She listened to us, and probably agreed with us, as she could not exactly say that Mrs. Curtis was wrong. She said she would look into this and we should not worry.

In this situation I am the story of forming a relationship with an adult who can be an ally. In that role I communicated my point of view effectively. The adult in the story listened to my ideas.

At the Washington, DC, CLE, these Journey Line stories were shared using the Digital Video Booth pedagogy.

WORLD CAFÉ

There are multiple purposes of the World Café. The process fosters Gracious Space and it draws on diverse perspectives while supporting equitable access/participation. The salon atmosphere of the World Café is built around participant movement among and across tables and the ideas being discussed at each.

Theoretical Underpinnings

The World Café is a process that provides opportunities for people to synthesize, deconstruct, or build upon distinct ideas related to a common topic or theme. Participant movement promotes constructive learning principles because it is interactive and relies on generating input from diverse people around multiple topics. World Cafés are complex and authentic experiential learning.

Outcome

The outcomes of World Café are to design and implement an interactive process in which the participants co-construct understanding and knowledge through iterative experiences with diverse participants and perspectives.

Process

As with all processes, the specific implementation of the World Café should be based on the principles and general design but be customized for use by facilitators to achieve outcomes. It is important to understand the role of the World Café facilitators. The facilitators' role is to see that the guidelines for dialogue and engagement are put into action. It is not the specific form but living the spirit of the guidelines that matters. Hosting a World Café requires thoughtfulness, artistry, and care. The World Café facilitators can make the difference between an interesting conversation and a breakthrough in thinking. The responsibilities of the World Café facilitators are to

- work with the planning team to determine the purpose of the World Café and decide who should be invited to the gathering.
- be creative in adapting the World Café guidelines so they meet the unique needs of the specific situation.
- name the World Café in a way appropriate to its purpose and to help frame the invitation.
- create a comfortable environment by working with others.
- design an appropriate question with the World Café hosts; when constructing a *powerful question*, ask yourself the following questions:
  o Is it simple and clear?
  o Is it thought provoking?
  o Does it generate energy?
  o Does it focus on collective inquiry?
  o Does it surface any unconscious assumptions?
  o Does it open new possibilities?
  o Does it seek what is useful?
- welcome the participants as they enter.
- explain the purpose of the gathering.
- pose the question or themes for rounds of conversation, and make sure that the question is visible to everyone.
- explain the World Café guidelines and etiquette by exhibiting on an overhead, flipchart, on cards at each table, or via another visual aid.
- explain how the logistics of the World Café will work, including the role of the "table host"—the volunteer who remains at his or her table at the end of the first round to welcome newcomers, then circulates among tables during the conversations and encourages everyone to participate throughout the exchange.
- remind people to make notes, doodles, or drawings of key ideas.
- let people know, in a gentle way, when it is time to move and begin a new round of conversation.
- make sure key insights are recorded visually or gathered and posted, when possible.

Implementation

In preparation for World Café, each table is provided with a large sheet of poster paper for participants to write on. If you want to go "all out," you can set up a World Café environment with tablecloths, flowers, and/or refreshments. There is typically a facilitator/host at each table. However, it is up to you whether or not the table host remains for all conversation rounds.

With preparations in place, World Café begins with groups of four to six members joined in conversation clusters and proceeds as follows:

- There will be three progressive rounds of conversation of approximately 8–12 minutes each, with the questions/topics co-designed with hosts of each table.
- Questions, issues, or thoughts that pertain to the designated topic are explored.
- Hosts and members write, doodle, and draw key ideas on the paper in the center of the group at each conversation cluster table. Group members may take notes for later reference.
- Upon completing the initial round of conversation, one person remains at the table as the "host" while the others become travelers or "ambassadors of meaning." The travelers move to other tables to cross-pollinate key ideas and questions into new conversations that may give greater meaning to rounds of conversation to follow.
- Table hosts should welcome the new guests and briefly share the main ideas, themes, and questions of the initial conversation. Guests should link and connect ideas coming from their previous table conversations—listening carefully and building on each other's contributions.
- If cohort members move and engage in several rounds of conversation, it will provide opportunities for ideas, questions, and themes to begin to link and connect.
- A conversation among the whole group is initiated after three rounds of World Café conversations. This whole-group conversation is a town meeting–style conversation in which patterns can be identified, collective knowledge is "harvested," and possibilities for new and applied meanings emerge.

WORLD CAFÉ ETIQUETTE
Focus on what matters.
Contribute your thinking.
Speak your mind.
Listen to understand.
Link and connect ideas.
Listen together for insights and deeper questions.
Play, Doodle, Draw—writing on the paper is important!

World Café in Action

In Community Learning Exchanges, we have used the World Café in various settings. The World Café fosters sharing and interactivity among CLE participants.

For more information, visit www.theworldcafe.com.

World Café Examples

World Cafés are used to provide feedback on team action plans.

LEARNING WALKS

The physical act of having a side-by-side conversation rather than a face-to-face conversation changes the way people relate. This offers a process for active practice of our talk about dialogue as a process for transforming our reality. In addition, it offers something we rarely do in meetings—exercise and get fresh air. This process by itself freshens our perspectives, sharpens our thinking, and adds a way of learning from others not often considered as vital in our busy schedules.

Learning Walks were inspired by the work of Miles Horton and the Highlander Center in New Market, Tennessee. Horton famously engaged in walking conversations with Paulo Freire. A subsequent book of their conversations was called *We Make the Road by Walking*. The meanings behind the title include the principle of solutions driven by local people and the wisdom and assets they possess. The title also has a physical meaning—walking itself is a pedagogy for learning.

Meetings are usually held in spaces that have a history or a visual appeal that can be inspiring. Learning Walks focused around a guiding question can help people feel open and compelled to engage in conversations. Additionally, a collateral outcome of this pedagogy is that one gains a further learning about the physical space that is being occupied.

Process

Prior to a Learning Walk, offer a guiding question that helps the learning pair engage in a conversation. The question is generated by what has happened in the meeting up to that point. Besides a guiding question, a Web activity where individuals each hold information from site visits, personal stories, readings, and so on, and then take turns sharing can be useful.

Grouping

Groups are preferably pairs but can also be trios. Although larger groups can work, experience has shown that Learning Walks tend to be more effective when limited to two people per group.

Space

Learning Walks need adequate space, inside or outside, to be most effective. The walks should take place where there is enough space to provide some privacy to the participants for uninterrupted conversation.

Recording

Lessons and learning from the conversations do not need to be recorded formally. However, there may be times where another person records the Learning Walk conversations via video, audio, or simple notes. This can be done in order to formalize and share the learning with others.

References and Further Readings

Balutski, N., Militello, M., Janson, C., Benham, M., & Francis, L. (2014, April). *InQuiry: A research methodology for Indigenous communities.* Paper presented at the World Indigenous Peoples' Conference in Education Conference, Honolulu, Hawaii.

Brown, J., & Isaacs, D. (2005). *The World Café: Shaping our futures through conversations that matter.* San Francisco, CA: Berrett-Koehler.

Brown, S. (2006). A match made in heaven: A marginalized methodology for studying the marginalized. *Quality & Quantity, 40,* 361–382.

Freire, P. (1997). *Pedagogy of the oppressed.* New York, NY: Continuum.

Guajardo, F., & Guajardo, M. (2013). The power of Platica. *Reflections: A Journal of Public Rhetoric, Civic Writing, and Service Learning, 13*(1), 159–164.

Horton, M., Freire, P., Bell, B., Gaventa, J., & Peters, J. (1990). *We make the road by walking: Conversations on education and social change.* Philadelphia, PA: Temple University Press.

Hughes, P., & Grace, B. (2010). *Gracious Space: A practical guide to working together* (2nd ed.). Seattle, WA: Center for Ethical Leadership.

Militello, M., & Benham, M. (2010). "Sorting out" collective leadership: How Q–methodology can be used to evaluate leadership development. *Leadership Quarterly, 21*(4), 620–632.

Militello, M., & Janson, C. (2015). *InQuiry: Finally an evaluation methodology of the people, for the people.* Unpublished manuscript.

Militello, M., Janson, C., Guajardo, E., & Militello, D. (2014). *Community Learning Exchange annual report.* Washington, DC: Institute for Educational Leadership.

Militello, M., Janson, C., & Militello, D. (2014). *InQuiry: A participant inclusive process for leadership and community development.* Paper presented at the New Zealand Educational Administration and Leadership Society Annual Conference, Wellington, New Zealand.

Schon, D. (1983). *The reflective practitioner.* New York, NY: Basic Books.

Watts, S., & Stenner, P. (2012). *Doing Q methodological research: Theory, method and interpretation.* Thousand Oaks, CA: Sage.

Weissglass, J. (1990). Constructivist listening for empowerment and change. *The Educational Forum, 50*(4), 351–370.

8

DYNAMIC-CRITICAL PEDAGOGIES WITH AND IN COMMUNITY

Communities matter. Like families, communities have their own ecology, spirit, dynamic, and flow. Much of our community work is anchored in the principles of family. Communities too often only rally around events of celebration or disaster. Recent events provide examples of communities gathering and galvanizing around injustices.

The purpose of a democracy is to create conditions for and to maintain and sustain healthy communities. As the American Republic took shape in the eighteenth and nineteenth centuries, the identity of the country was shaped by the concept of the individual, and individualism even became the American mythology. Events of the twentieth century such as world wars and the Great Depression brought the country together, and community took on different meaning. It gained prominence, next to the popular concept of the individual. Today communities are lived in the local—there has been a loss of the macro understanding of community on the national or global levels. Communities, mico or macro, must return to roots of engaging a diverse and intergenerational group of people who learn together. This is a place of consciousness for communities, a place where the local is honored, where outsiders are welcomed, and where people work together to harness local wisdom to create healthy places to live.

This chapter highlights a set of "pedagogies with and in community," specific strategies to engage with and in communities. Each pedagogy honors local context and expertise and is designed for immediate implementation. After the pedagogy is described, we provide an example of the pedagogy in action—an account of its use in a national or local CLE. Finally, we highlight links to videos for you to *see* the pedagogy in action. The video links can be found in *Video Links* categorized by the specific pedagogies.

DIGITAL ENGAGEMENT

We live in a time when we can meld new technologies with traditional storytelling rituals. Digital skills are now central to work and life, and multimedia technologies offer rich, diverse, and accessible avenues for self-expression. With new advances in Web 2.0 technologies (e.g., social networking, wikis, blogs, avatars, Second Life), data visualization has become normal practice. We use technology as a pedagogy to engage, research, and share. Here we highlight three specific Digital Engagement strategies we employ as pedagogies.

Digital Storytelling

Digital Storytelling has been a useful tool to engage people and capture voices. This pedagogy allows participants to be reflective, appreciate, and learn from others, and engage in public learning. Digital storytelling is about the process of crafting the story, not about the technology. The process that allows participants to be reflective, appreciative of others, and action oriented. This triumvirate can be investigated in all three ecologies of knowing: self, organization, and community. We use digital stories to craft individual, team, and organizational stories.

DigiHunt

The DigiHunt is an extension of the standard scavenger hunt, but framed within a group learning and collaborative dynamic that introduces participants to the local ecology while seeking to create moments of synthesis and understanding between participants and communities. In naming the DigiHunt, our idea is to utilize digital technology (e.g., smartphones, computers, cloud-based social media) to assist with the process and presentation. The first use of the DigiHunt for a CLE was during the Wisconsin–Minneapolis collaborative exchange. Groups moved through stations established on the grounds of the gathering while seeking "clues" as a group. This photo hunt led to the next incarnation at the San Marcos CLE, where the DigiHunt concept was fully explored as part of the CLE learning process. The DigiHunt has been used at subsequent gatherings, in graduate seminars, and professional development activities.

Planning DigiHunt

Leading up to the DigiHunt, local CLE teams spend time thinking out how the hunt will proceed and how it fits with the overall theme and mission of the CLE. There are four actions within the planning stage of the DigiHunt:

- **Establish the questions:** The planning team formulates between 8 and 10 questions based on the theme of the gathering. These questions are designed to engage participants in meaning-making while exploring the local ecology.

- **Establish the locations:** Where is everyone going? How long will it take them to get there and back? These are important questions to establish when thinking about the logistics of the activity in relation to the entire CLE experience. An example is the CLE hosted in San Marcos during the summer of 2013. Summers in Central Texas are very hot, therefore locations could not be too far for people to travel in a reasonable amount of time outside. The planning team made the decision to host each of the locations indoors, so teams would have the chance to cool off.
- **Create the teams:** How are people paired together? By home team? A random collection? Any of these options are fine, but some thought should go into how teams are organized prior to the hunt.
- **Technology:** Thought should be given to how the DigiHunt will be utilized. Most participants have some technological capacity, but this should not imply that everyone will have the same level of skill with uploading or downloading pictures. In one DigiHunt, more than an hour was spent trying to download photos to a single computer for the presentation phase. In another, not everyone was able to gain access to the social media platform we selected for presentations. Careful consideration needs to be made in how the technology will be integrated into the CLE so it does not detract from the overall experience.

The Hunt

The DigiHunt itself is a two- to three-hour activity that includes instructions, the hunt, and the presentation. For the hunt, teams work together to make meaning of questions and find representations of each question during their walk around the local community. Locations could include areas of significance for local community members, and the activity should be a way for participants to both be outside and to engage in the local ecology. Each of the team members must be present in at least one of the photo shots to ensure the whole team is represented. Teams should capture answers to each of the questions using a phone, camera, or other device deemed appropriate for the sharing and presentation portion of the activity.

- **Presentation:** There are a number of options for sharing the DigiHunt with the CLE participants. This decision should also be thought out in the planning stage; teams can share photos/answers one by one, or possibly select just one photo to summarize the experience if time is a consideration. The best approach is both sharing the photos and creating a collaborative piece to explain the experience of the hunt. This can be a song, a skit, or a poem, which can draw out another aspect of the team collaboration.
- **Purpose:** The purpose of the DigiHunt revolves around group meaning making. The necessity of understanding local context and local ecology is

critical to the work of the CLEs. The concepts of exploration and collaboration are key components to learning in public, and the digital representation means that the work has the ability to be shared beyond the scope of the CLE.

DigiHunt Example 1: Concepts in the Community

- **Destination:** Each team's destination is located on the outside of the folder.
- **Instructions:** Teams head toward the destination written on their folder. Teams evaluate the given clues and use whatever means at their disposal to capture an image/representation of the clues (e.g., using a smart phone, iPod, digital camera).
  o For each of the clues, every team member must be included in the image/representation (or in the process). At least one image needs to have the destination included in it.
  o Provide a time to complete tasks and people to contact for assistance.
  o There are no right answers for the clues, only your answers and your imagination.
- **Final representation/product:** Teams receive instruction/a guiding question for the final product/presentation to be delivered via website, social media account, or thumb drive.
- **Clues:** Following are suggestions for clues that might be given:

1. An act of power	6. Equity and compensation
2. A practice of policy	7. Evidence of the nature of work
3. Gracious Space	8. Evidence of the spirit of place
4. Evidence of dignity	9. The character of structures
5. A gift/impact of education	

Special Instructions: Engage another group and ask for an example of how they are experiencing the tension between the mechanical/technical and the social, then capture the strategy (image) that they are using to work through the tension. Once participants have completed the task, they can head back and be ready to present/share at the established time.

DigiHunt Example 2: Classroom Concepts

This exercise is designed to help identify and bring the concepts from the readings and coursework to practice and help participants develop a deeper understanding. It is a hybrid activity that finds its roots in the exploratory learning activities of the scavenger hunt, show-and-tell, and using digital tools for play.

Participants identify and provide responses to the given questions by using a digital camera, phone, or a recorder to capture the observables. There is not one right answer to any of these questions, so instruct participants to not let the search for certainty get in the way of learning. Questions do not need to be answered in a linear format; instead, participants can construct a story or interview or arrange images and/or frames to answer the collective questions. Any articles or other materials given to help guide this exercise also help frame the learning, while the activity itself will help inform the pedagogy.

The final product should not be more than three minutes long and can be produced on iMovie, PowerPoint, or similar software. Be sure final video products are saved through a standard platform, such as MP3 or MP4, when exported to facilitate the viewing process.

- **Political concepts:** Following are political concepts of the exercise:
  o Within your organization, where is the power situated? Capture it digitally.
  o Show how decisions are made in your organization.
  o Identify and capture conflict at the workplace.
  o Capture images of democracy at work.
- **Race:** Following are race-related elements of the exercise:
  o Find evidence of historical racial injustices. Capture diversity at work.
  o Capture nature at work.
  o Capture and display deficit ideology and practice at work.
- **Gender:** Following are gender-related elements of the exercise:
  o Capture gender equity at work.
  o Capture evidence that challenge gender equity.
- **Political Imagination**
  o Identify community assets.
  o Where do you find your power source (personally, organizationally or community)?
  o Identify and display three assets at your work life: at the personal, organizational and community level.
  o Capture and demonstrate evidence of advocacy at work.
  o Find evidence of attempts at being ecologically responsive and/or sustainable.

Video Booth

Photo booths are a way to capture memories of candid moments in social settings. Similarly, the Video Booth is design to engage participants through candid insights into a process or theme. The Video Booth offers a safe space for honest offerings or insights. Participants are made aware that the videos will be used later for additional public learning.

- **Equipment and expertise:** Most people are intimidated when it comes to the creation of videos. We have learned to rely on the technological expertise of participants themselves. In any gathering, there are bound to be participants who know how to engage in video editing. Along the way, we have learned a few things:

  o Use quiet places to record. Too often, we cannot use video because the voices cannot be heard.
  o Use well-lighted places to record. Good lighting matters in video production.
  o Equipment:

    - A good external microphone used in conjunction with a quiet recording space will ensure you capture the audio that is needed.
    - A portable lighting station can also be helpful.
    - Video editing software: All computers now come with free video editing software. PCs come loaded with MovieMaker and Apple computers with iMovie.

  o Participant release forms: Be sure to provide and collect signed consent forms for video production. We provide an example of a release form in the *Appendix*.

Digital Engagement in Action

Video cameras are ubiquitous. Just about everyone has a camera these days, and there is always someone listening and recording. We have found that it is very important to record virtually every CLE activity and believe that recordings should be used for learning in public in real time. It is common practice to share digital products during a CLE. The examples below highlight how we implement digital tools at CLEs.

Digital Engagement Examples

We have used Digital Storytelling to provide a compilation of learning at an event. To see the videos visit the *Video Links* section on Digital Engagement.

In Central Texas, participants engaged in a *DigiHunt* in downtown San Marcos. They worked in teams to follow clues and to record visual representations of their findings with smartphones. The visuals were shared in two ways: (a) a Tumblr account was created to share photos and videos in real-time and (b) teams used the photos and videos to create a short presentation for the larger group.

We have used Video Booths at a number of CLEs. For example, we asked participants: *What is your recipe for change?* The audience responded in real time, online, to their own recipe for community change. Then, we asked participants to relate the recipe to their work in the community.

On another occasion, we asked participants: *What is your gift?* Audience members recorded personal reflections of their own gifts.

In both of the above cases, videos were viewed publically and the audience was asked to respond. See the *Video Links*.

PERFORMANCE: MUSIC, POETRY, DANCE, AND ART

The power of music to motivate and animate is undisputed. The "sound track" of any CLE may actually use music or, through interactions, the music of dialogue helps infuse the setting with a spirit. Music and other forms of artistic expression can be welcoming and therapeutic for participants. We have used a number of performance pedagogies in CLEs, including local performances, open mic night, poster/t-shirt art, even specific music and art, and duet poems. We provide an overview for these below with an in-depth set of instructions for duet poems.

Local Performances

At many Community Learning Exchanges, we invite local performers. Often this is done to kick off a CLE or as dinner time entertainment. Local musicians and artists are invited to share their talents and their cultural attributes.

Open Mic Night

Time and space are provided at CLEs for attendees to share any kind of performance they would like. Participants often bring musical instruments with them to CLEs. It is helpful to have an emcee for the Open Mic to keep things flowing.

Poster/T-Shirt Art

Participants (individuals and teams) often provide opportunities to capture thoughts, action plans, or representations of knowledge on poster paper or blank t-shirts. Here, we simply provide materials (e.g., poster paper, markers, blank white t-shirts, fabric paint), and the participants create amazing artistic products.

Event-Specific Music and Art

There have been several occasions where hosts and/or participants have created a unique CLE-specific piece of art or music. For artwork, planners can provide a large canvas and paint for participants to add collectively to over time. Others may wish to create a poem or song that represents the work being done together.

Duet Poems

Duet poems come in multiple forms and can be written by a single person to represent two points of view, as if there is a conversation. Most of us are familiar with singing duets and taking turns to sing. In the case of the duet poems, the writers perform the poem as if taking turns.

Duet Poem Detail

- **Writing:** The poem duet is co-constructed by two persons in a "call-and-response" format—typically speaking to the same reality or identity from two points of view. The writers can choose to repeat a portion as a repetitive refrain or chorus. In the tradition of speaking one's truth and naming one's reality, the poems are about identity—personal and collective—and one's sense of self in a society.
- **Presentation:** Decide whether to position participants looking toward the audience or talking to each other. Participants should practice the reading with inflection and strong voices, and introduce themselves and the poem's title to the audience if the poem has a title. Lastly, they should read and/or perform the poem.

Duet Poem Example

Following is an example of a Duet Poem that was created by two participants at the North Carolina Community Learning Exchange.

On the Question of Identity

Person 1	*Person 2*
They ask me to write about being a black woman And I think and think very seriously will they understand Are you sure you want to travel in my size 8 shoes Think before you answer it's a life I did not choose	They ask me to write about being a black woman And I think and think very seriously will they understand Are you sure you want to travel in my size 8 shoes Think before you answer it's a life I did not choose
(1) When I was born I had ten fingers and toes, a head full of hair and a wide nose As I grew I began to do things like walk talk write and sing but could never understand this one little thing Still to this day it still makes me ponder how you can demean being a baby momma That's what I am a giver of life and somehow ended up being a wife But all that can't change how I was born	(2) When I was born I was their first girl The one they hoped would help change the world As I grew I dreamed of success I was ready for the world and all of its tests I am still working on my goals I have to play many roles I am a loving, supportive wife My best deed thus far was giving Taylor and Reggie life But all that can't change how I was born

(3) Life can teach me lessons whether I'm ready or not
Feeling like I have so much to prove to Mr. Big Shot
Trying to get as much education in this big head of mine
So I won't end up smelling of alcohol in the unemployment line
Or rushing to the mailbox monthly on the first or third day
Looking straight-ahead forgetting about the people I have to pay
None of the aforementioned pertains to my personal situation
But because of what I am on the outside it's so many people's observation
Do I try to prove them wrong and say hey wait I do have a brain
Or will that just justify the reason why I'm sometimes called insane
But all that can't change how I was born

(4) Life did teach me lessons whether I was ready or not
I always have to prove how I got what I got
They see the big house, immaculate yard and fancy truck
However, they don't understand it didn't happen by luck.
They were not there when I had to leave school because my parent didn't have the money
The naysayers may have even thought it was the end of my journey
Many don't understand how education was my only ticket out
They only had their snickering laughs and many doubts
I had to struggle to rebound and start with a new plan
Thankful that God had already promised me a winning hand
But all that can't change how I was born

(5) Oh no times have definitely changed there are far more advancements
But some didn't get that memo what happened to my handful of chances
Being a black woman do you really want to know
What goes through my mind or just the part I have to show
If you can't beat em join em but what if you are denied
Entry into this world by being judged and ostracized
Some others are put on a pedestal with their Barbie like figure
Look at me and my hips, wide enough for the babies I had to deliver
We all look alike, eat watermelon and love some fried chicken
Beat our kids, look for handouts so many others I could mention
At least that's what you think or so you have been taught or told
Close your eyes and imagine your loved ones being sold
Yeah yeah yeah I know it's the same old story
But the strength I have, my God gets all the glory
If you walk a mile in my shoes you still wouldn't understand
How it makes me feel to be thought of as less than my fellow man
But all that can't change how I was born

(6) Times have changed and there are far more advancements
Some still just refuse to honor our chances
Being a black woman sometimes seems like a curse
When some people see us they just assume the worse
They see the braids, natural hair and weave
They automatically think we can't achieve
Society tries to prove that color doesn't matter
However, we all know it is the root of the battle
Look at the President of The United States
Never has a leader been so disrespected and greeted with such hate
I now understand what my Grandma meant about having burdens to bare
Trying to live in a world that just doesn't seem fair
Yet I keep trying to grow and succeed
Praying that society won't judge me by my color but by my good deeds
But all that can't change how I was born

(7) Trying to teach someone to see you for who you really are
Is the dumbest thing I've heard in my life so far
Having a scarlet letter on your back in a crowd so deep
Some live by the notion you sow what you reap
Often people say what's done in the dark will surely come to the light
What's in your heart will show although you try to hide it with all of your might
Trying to toe that line do you even know what's right
You can't fool em all even blind people have a sense of sight
They ask me to write about being a black woman
And I think and think very seriously will they understand
No is my answer because they have a bird in the hand
Are you sure you want to travel in my size 8 shoes
Think before you answer it's a life I did not choose

(8) They say don't judge a book by its cover
Yet we don't take the time to truly get to know each other
We preach that education is the key
However, when are we going to see the equity
The state of North Carolina released its charter school cap
Makes you wonder if they really want to close the achievement gap
Public schools are almost once again segregated
Makes the work of our ancestors look suffocated
I know some things are not like they seem
Just like Martin Luther King I still have a dream
Are you sure you want to travel in my size 8 shoes
Think before you answer it's a life I did not choose

Performance in Action

Performances, art, and music have become staples at Community Learning Exchanges. Many of the performances began informally. Over time, we have come to realize the importance of formally embracing the arts into our work.

Performance Examples

Local performers and artist have always been invited to CLE events. For example, at many CLEs, local elders hold a ceremony to welcome us to the land where their ancestors have lived for hundreds of years.

Open Mic Nights are a popular way for participants to share their talents. See the *Video Links* to watch a video from the Central Texas CLE—the voice-over on the video is a poem written and performed by a CLE participant.

At the Jacksonville CLE, participants had the opportunity to add to a collective piece of art. The final painting was displayed at the closing Circle (see photos in Chapter 9).

At the Jacksonville, Florida, CLE, a local planning committee member worked with friends to write and record a theme song for the CLE. See the *Video Links* to watch a performance of the song that opened the CLE.

T-shirts have been used as a way for groups to represent a common theme. Pictured are T-shirts created at the Seattle and Hawaii CLEs (see Figure 9.2). Groups were assigned based on perspectives they mutually held. Each group created an image and slogan for their new "family."

The *Video Links* contain a link to a reflection poem that was written by a participant at the conclusion of the Montana CLE. The participant set the poem to music and images. The video was played at the CLE closing ceremony.

COMMUNITY SITE VISITS

Place-based learning, which occurs in and with the community in which an organization or school is situated, is vital to constructing outcomes that are culturally consonant and useful to all constituents. Community or site visits can take multiple forms but should be designed to foster reciprocity. The visitors need roles and responsibilities with clear protocols and processes so that they may interact in community spaces in ways that foster Gracious Space and achieve learning outcomes.

Authentic place-based learning answers this question based on Dewey's (1963) inquiry: How can the stories of this place and the experience in this place be a *moving force for change* in our current situations? How can you "tell" the story of this place through experiences of the participants (visitors)? Thus, the Community Site Visits are co-constructed with the community experts being informative as well as experiential. They start with an essential question and incorporate key pedagogical elements of the CLE (mini-opening Circle, Gracious Space, learning walks and talks, critical conversations). The visit should inform the participants about the spirit and historical facts of the place; it should stimulate the participants to connect the experience to the organizational purpose with a focus on connecting work in organizations and schools to the community spirit and settings.

As we all take responsibility for holding the sacred trust of educating and loving our children into their futures, these are our guiding questions:

- How does your story and history inform this experience and guide your development as an advocate for healing in your community?
- What is the power source fueling this place, work, or idea?
- What does leadership for community work and action/advocacy look like?

Outcomes

The outcomes for the community site visits differ for each role in the learning exchange. Participants, facilitators, and experts should seek particular outcomes, as defined in the following.

All participants will be able to

- fully engage in inquiry and experiential learning based on specific site history and information
- connect stories of origin and identity to the stories of this site
- connect the purpose of community visit to overall purposes/goals
- connect stories of the site to home communities

Community visit facilitator(s) will be able to:

- develop specific outcomes for site visits
- prepare an experience (and specific agenda) for the community site visit that includes CLE pedagogies and honors the community expert's information and experience

Community experts will be able to:

- look for connections between the purpose/goal of the community visit and the stories of place
- pose questions
- engage with the site visit facilitator(s) to develop processes for the site visit that inform and engage, that is, that engage more through *doing* than through *telling*

Preparation

- Provide timeline, overview, readings, and photos for each group as applicable to the site visit.
- Ask community experts to help you understand the most important events and implications and the right materials for your group.
- Consider how the group will "record" the experience and be ready to share with others.
- Assign roles for map "drawer" as situation dictates.
  - o Artist(s)/illustrator(s) who draw the experience
  - o Photographer(s)
  - o Videographer
  - o Note-taker(s) and questioner(s) of experts
  - o Collector(s) of additional questions needing to be addressed
  - o Collector(s) of information or objects
  - o Process observer(s) who not only take notes on what was "visited" but are asking provocative questions of fellow participants: What are you observing? What are you feeling? What does this cause you to think about?

CLE Implementation

There are two keys to a successful community site visit: (a) site selection and (b) site collaboration. Site visit organizers should allocate the necessary time and space to research, visit, and collaborate with community members in order to identify an appropriate place for a site visit. Site visits are predicated on learning from one another. As such, organizers must identify sites that have a spirit of sharing and learning. A common shortcoming of a site visit is the notion that visitors want to only listen to the hosts "talk." Site visits should be organized around the principles of conversations.

Possible Agenda

- **Mini-opening Circle (may or may not include the community experts):** Design an opening question that relates to the purpose of the community visit *and* the people in the group.
- **Gracious Space:** How have you accounted for Gracious Space implicitly (or explicitly)? How is this a setting and a spirit to invite the stranger and learn in public?
- **Essential or inquiry question:** Remind all participants of the guiding questions, and use an inquiry stance.
  - o What do you observe?
  - o What do you feel?
  - o What do you know and what did you learn?
  - o What does this mean?
- **Experiential learning for community visit:** This will depend on the information, the experts, the places, and so on. Here are some ideas for constructing this so it is experiential:
  - o What do folks already know? What do they want to know? Followed at the end with what did you learn?
  - o Divide the group up to attend different site visit agenda items.
  - o Have paired teams walk certain place(s) on the site.
  - o Provide music and art experiences.
  - o Implement a town hall with community expert(s).
- **Closing Circle:** What resonates with you the most in this community site and how will that inform your/our work?
- **Reflection and Debriefing:**
  - o What are the contradictions of the place?
  - o What does the place tell about the goals and/or purpose of the community visit?
  - o What surprises or "aha" moments did you have during this community visit?
  - o What power does this give you for advocacy in your community?

One final note: We often break teams up so that there are representatives from various teams on each of the site visits. We have used the reflection/debriefing time to allow for team sharing from the site visits.

Community Site Visits in Action

In Community Learning Exchanges, we have used community site visits as a strategy to understand the host city or place. The community visits allow participants from around the country to "see" other organizations that have their own unique set of assets and barriers to their work.

Community Site Visit Examples

In Washington, DC, participants visited five different organizations that supported advocacy for persons with disabilities (the focus of the DC CLE):

1. Gallaudet Campus and Museums
2. Capital City Public Charter School, Washington, DC.
3. Latin American Youth Center
4. Autistic Self-Advocacy Network at National Youth Transitions Center
5. Adaptive Services Division of MLK Library

During the North Carolina CLE, participants went to one of four site visits (see *Video Links*). Participants at each site heard stories from local witnesses to events. In Williamston, participants re-enacted a march through downtown, singing songs of freedom along the way.

At the Hawaii CLE, participants engaged in *work* at a site visit. The Maó farm site visit included an early morning drive for a number of participants who experienced the work on a youth-led organic farm (see *Video Links*).

Works in Progress

We have learned from other organizations and convenings where Community Learning Exchange pedagogies or CLE-like pedagogies are engaged. Participants engaged in a Works in Progress (WIP) activity at a recent North Dakota Study Group. Their call was simple—*we encourage you to think about the work you are currently doing, get valuable feedback, and take your ideas to the next level in a small group setting.*

People convene a Work in Progress when they have been working on or thinking about a question, problem, or concern and want to hear the ideas of others who share this interest. Typically, WIP conveners spend the first 10–15 minutes of a WIP session explaining their question before opening up the conversation for the ideas and suggestions of others. The WIP is generally a place for exploring ideas and getting different points of view, rather than a place for presenting finished work.

Participants can expect anywhere from 3 to 25 people in a presentation. Even a small number can give valuable feedback. When not presenting, participants are encouraged to attend other WIP presentations that will be going on simultaneously.

Works in Progress in Action

The Works in Progress (WIP) are similar to the Gallery Walks that were previously described in a number of the CLE pedagogies. The WIP can be also be planned as an Action Plan, or it can be a testing ground for a new idea.

Works in Progress Examples

At the 2015 North Dakota Study Group hosted in South Texas, a number of WIP topics were presented and feedback provided, including the following:

1. How do we build a national Save Our Schools Movement?
2. What does a beginning progressive teacher look like?
3. How can the "Bracero" oral history project in South Texas be replicated in other communities?
4. How can we have an impact on the next iteration of the Elementary Secondary School Education Act?

PLAY

Play is a term often relegated to children or to the sophomoric attitudes of adults. However, play is an important aspect of work. The most famous story of play is of the self-imposed knight-errant Don Quixote. Quixote's search for righteousness vis-à-vis chivalrous idealism is confounded by his delusions. His journey is riddled with folly—from fighting windmills he thinks are sword-wielding knights, to riding a donkey he believes to be a regal steed, to wearing a wash basin as a helmet he considers to have the power of invulnerability. There are lessons to be learned through play and folly. Organizational theorist James March implores people and organizations to maintain balance between being overly *techno-rationale* and play. March denotes this as *exploitation*, seeking solutions that are efficient and reliable, and a *technology of foolishness*. March also infers that *exploration* is about risk taking, experimentation, and variation.

Play is about fellowship and community, and it is a powerful bond between people as well as between people and places. A lasting, thoughtful solution to a problem may be found in rational *and* non-rational places. Creating space for each is the focus of the play pedagogy.

Examples of Play in Practice

Play can take many forms. It can be most powerful when it incorporates the theme being discussed and is representative of the convening space and location.

Semi-structured, intentional play can take many forms. This pedagogy needs a time allotment in the agenda. It can be as simple as a volleyball game or as complex as learning a new game or sport. On a cautionary note, there may be participants who do not want to, or are unable to, participate in a physical activity. We have also come to realize that there must be choices during the play pedagogy. For instance, in Montana, attendees could learn how to drum rather than play Double Ball, if they chose.

Play in Action

Play has become an important feature in the Community Learning Exchange. Play did not begin as a formal pedagogy at the CLEs. Rather, we discovered how "breaks" in the work became important extensions of the work itself. We discovered how new ideas and new networks around the work developed during times of play.

Play Examples

On a chilly October evening in Whitakers, North Carolina, convening organizers provided attendees with ingredients for s'mores. Beside a campfire, participants talked, sang, and ate. Evening events such as the campfire have become a hallmark to CLEs because of the learning that takes place.

Elders at the Salish-Kootnai Community College in Montana taught a sport called "Double Ball" to convening attendees. Learning the game included learning the historical development of the game as well as the rationale for specific rules, such as the rule that men could not hit women with the sticks, but woman could hit men with impunity.

Organizers in Jacksonville, Florida, brought convening attendees to historical St. Augustine. Participants spend the morning on the beach—playing football, learning to surf, or just walking and talking with others. Some attendees were able to see and feel the Atlantic Ocean for the very first time.

COMMUNITY MAPPING

Communities, especially racially segregated communities with high poverty rates, are under scrutiny. Too often, communities are viewed with a deficient lens. One needs to ask the question, What is wrong with the community?

- Is the housing dilapidated?
- Are crime, incarceration, and violence rates extremely high?
- Are schools inadequately serving students?
- Is infrastructure lacking?

Such questions cannot be ignored. However, despite issues that may characterize the community as deficient, the script can be flipped by asking a key question focused on the whole of the community: How can we use an asset frame to analyze communities even if there are serious issues? Realistically, any hope of rebuilding healthy communities must address community issues, but any community mapping process directed at change can only be successful if it begins with identifying local assets—the people, places, and activities that already generate and inspire hope.

Community mapping is a process that relies on the power of place as the text. The process seeks to identify and analyze both the assets and issues within a community, the size of which can range from a small neighborhood to a large city. The map is typically connected to a specific geographical area. The objective is to name specific assets and issues in order to help the community create plans for change-based action. These principles guide the mapping process and any products that result from engagement in the process: (a) school and community mapping reflect the criteria for a strong experience—continuity and interaction (vis-à-vis John Dewey's work); thus, mapping is deep and sustained over time, encouraging continuity, so as to shift patterns and relationships; (b) the mapping process fosters reciprocity between and among the participants as well as between the participants and the community; and (c) mapping emanates from a question or inquiry and a need to know. In these ways, mapping is both a principle-based and strategic process for engaging participants in learning about a school and/or community and about each other.

A key attribute of effective mapping is reciprocity. Thus, the mapping process hinges on relationships between the mappers and with the community or school persons. Individuals (typically persons who come to the community as allies) must build a strong rapport with community members and community organizations. Mappers need to listen to the community stories and to what they believe to be important about the community and its future. As a result of the relationships and shared storytelling, community leaders—whose perspective and expertise we count on—host teams of participants to create a community map (see the following details about forming teams and developing mapping directions for each team).

A map is certainly physical in mapping specific places in a community: businesses, landmarks, housing, community centers, and other key community institutions like schools, libraries, and churches. But a map can also be a narrative of the people's stories in the community. In sum, the map should produce a picture and a story about the community's assets and issues.

All persons participating in the community mapping experience need an introduction to community mapping. The facilitators should design and communicate a clear process for creating the map of the community. First, divide participants into teams. The teams then spend time visiting in the community—talking and walking (see CLE *Community Site Visits* pedagogy). The assets are not only physical but also assets of social capital, of people. By translating the assets to the issues that emerge, participants focus on the solution aspects of the mapping process by listening to the vision and voices of the residents.

Representational maps are created. In turn, the community mappers analyze the maps with the community residents. Working with the residents, participants engage in action planning (often using one of the CLE pedagogies such as *Logic Model for Action* or *Works in Progress*).

Notably, the process is not set in stone and should vary according to the context of the persons who are involved—parents, community members, professors, teachers, school leaders, graduate students, and/or grade school students. Each community mapping experience should inform subsequent "mappings," thus making it an iterative process. The process should recognize that the context is a critical variable to implementing community mapping. Facilitators need to clearly plan and communicate the mapping steps. We hope this introduction provides sufficient direction to try mapping. Like the implementation of all strategies, the first attempts involve some trial and error, but implementing and refining mapping processes are important.

These are guidelines, not hard and fast rules. These key questions are useful for all mapping plans:

- How have I/we accounted for reciprocity between and among community members?
- Who are the consultants/experts and the mapping teams?
- How is the mapping experience honoring the principles of interaction and continuity as the basis of the experience?
- How is the mapping grounded in an inquiry that relates to a need to know?

Step-by-Step Process

- **Step One—Form relationships with community:** Since relationships are the foundation of all change efforts in schools and communities, forming respectful, reciprocal, and responsive relationships is critical for all aspects of the mapping process. If a group, for example, is interested in mapping a particular community near a school, campus, or organization, then the mapping organizers should contact prospective participants, conduct pre-visits to the sites, and talk to the people about how their perspective or site can contribute to greater understanding.

The focus of the pre-mapping is to orient the prospective mapping participants to the purpose of the mapping, the probable procedure, the time frame, and so on. While this seems self-evident, it is often overlooked because it is time consuming for facilitators and planners. In their preparation, the mapping facilitators emphasize that the community consultants are the experts in the process, and learning from them is the reason for the mapping.

- **Step Two—Develop a community mapping process, inquiry question, and teams:** The facilitators carefully consider and decide on the purpose and the product of the mapping, and develop an inquiry approach based on these questions: What are you or your group interested in knowing? How will the mapping help answer your question? This may be a "wide-angle" question, such as: What are the major assets and issues in the community? Or it can be a narrower question: What are the major youth-serving organizations in the community? By community, we mean a designated geographical area.

  The mapping typically occurs with teams of three to six, so there must be attention to the purpose of the mapping, the roles they assume, the relationships they have with one another, how they will relate to persons in the mapping area, and how to authentically engage. The second set of key relationships occurs among the mappers. The facilitators should make provisions for those teams to engage in team building before engaging in mapping.

- **Step Three—Engage in community mapping:** Prior to the mapping, plan, plan, and then plan some more. Do a trial mapping if time permits, so that the facilitators feel confident in the process. The actual mapping never happens exactly like the plan. Therefore, it is important to have the materials and processes ready for the mappers to use so adjustments can be made as they engage. They each need a map with particular places to stop for pre-determined conversations, as well as suggested places they might stop to observe, learn, or converse.

    On the actual day of the mapping, there are typical time frames. Each of these steps requires thoughtful decisions and careful planning by facilitators:

    o   30 minutes for team building
    o   20–30 minutes for directions from facilitators
    o   15 minutes for teams to digest the directions and make plans for their particular mapping
    o   60–90 minutes for team mapping: walking, talking, meeting pre-determined community experts, photographing, collecting materials as appropriate, and so on
    o   30–60 minutes for initial debrief and production of a poster or other product to present to entire group

- **Step Four—Analyze results of community mapping:** To understand the learning from the mapping, participants analyze the themes of the mapping, what they experienced or felt, and what next steps might be. The analysis can take multiple forms, but a team poster or a visual representation of the experience organized in a "gallery" walk is one useful way. One person from each team remains with the poster to answer questions and take notes on conversation. This person should trade off with another so all have an opportunity to view the posters. All participants should look at the posters to glean common themes, find major community assets, and formulate questions. The participants can use Post-it notes or something similar to make notes on posters (some other mechanism could also be chosen). There could be, for example, a four-square debrief for each team's poster or representation, and participants can write on it:

Key Assets	Themes & Issues
Probing Questions	Affirmations

At the end of the Gallery Walk, the group should give feedback about the process so that subsequent mapping can be informed by that feedback. For this segment of the process, a possible strategy is using four-square feedback, using these key points in which the ▲ = what changes are needed:

Content ✚/▲	Themes & Issues
Process ✚/▲	Affirmations

- **Step Five—Action plan and follow-up:** This is typically where the mapping process may falter, so it is important that mapping facilitators clarify at the outset if the informational mapping is for a larger purpose. Introductory mapping (wide-lens mapping) may be helpful to plan for a deeper or more specific mapping experience, or if the next steps are quite different, such as incorporating the mapping in the curriculum of the school. The action plan depends on the purpose of the mapping and the group size, as well as other factors. If, for example, a community-based organization is planning the mapping, that organization then uses the assets to address a key issue and all the mappers contribute to the plan. If, for example, each team plans to use the mapping for a different purpose, there may be multiple action plans.

The analysis will likely include multiple assets and themes/issues. The next step is to gather these, analyze how they are related and how they interact, and prioritize—because typically all issues cannot be addressed at once. At this step, it is useful to get to the root causes of the issues and understand the factors over which the group actually has control or possibility of addressing—from insights gained in Steps 3–5 of the mapping process

In any case, the action plan should be based on an Asset Cycle of Inquiry: How can the assets be used to determine the goals and outcomes? What evidence will be used to determine interim progress?

Content +/△ How satisfied are you with the content? Process +/△	Questions??? Affirmations/Appreciations

---

Community Mapping in Action

In 2012–2013, the University Council of Educational Administration received a grant from the U.S. Department of Education to improve the preparation of school leaders for effectively supporting diverse learners. The work culminated in a set of six online learning modules. In the "Engaging Families and Communities" module, a "neighborhood walk" learning experience was developed. The free, online module includes protocols and readings. See the *Video Links* for module overviews and *Web Links* for additional information about the modules as well as resources from John McKnight and John Kretzmann.

Community Mapping Examples

Community mapping was used at Community Learning Exchanges in Brooklyn, New York, and Jacksonville, Florida. Parts of this pedagogy can be seen in digital stories from each Community Learning Exchange (see *Video Links*).

LOGIC MODEL FOR ACTION

During the Community Learning Exchanges reflections and understandings are important precursors for action. Logic model for action is what we do in practice once we have had experiences and time to reflect. It is the power behind CLE philosophies and protocols and the experience is tied to a responsibility for action. As Brazilian educator Paulo Freire (1997) said in his famous book *The Pedagogy of the Oppressed*,

> it is not enough for people to come together in dialogue in order to gain knowledge of their social reality. They must act together upon their environment in order to critically reflect upon their reality and to transform it through further action and critical reflection.

To move from reflection and understanding to action requires a specific set of guides. Our pedagogy of logic model for action is made up of a number of strategies to help the individual and the team take what they have learned home and to put it into meaningful action.

Step One: Discussion

Give participants 10 minutes to write a narrative that projects them into their future responsibility; they can use a computer if it is easier. The prompts for this narrative are as follows:

- Based on my reflection at this CLE, I now understand that ...
- I commit myself to ...

Appoint a note taker and facilitator to document all of the group's thinking. As a group, discuss these guiding questions:

- Based on the narratives of current understanding and commitments, what are the key ideas you want to share with your team?
- How did the CLE pedagogies support your reflection and learning?
- What ideas do you have (large and small) about transforming your organizational reality?
- Who are critical players (not present now) in your change efforts? How will you involve them?
- How will you do this—what are your action plan steps?

Step Two: Complete a Logic Model

After discussion, prepare a logic model for action. Keep in mind what you intend to do and how you intend to do it (i.e., what protocols might you use).

- Decide on a clear outcome or question that guides your action plan.
- Decide on the protocols that might support your actions.
- Include a section in your logic model for the kinds of internal and external supports you will need in order to carry out your action plan and how you will engage those supports.

We traditionally have provided a template of a logic model that was thorough and linear (see the following table).

CLE Logic Model

Goals to Evaluation Questions	Inputs/Means— Activities	Ends
SMART: Specific, Measurable, Action-oriented, Realistic, and Timed	In order to address the goals, the following inputs will be provided and activities will be accomplished.	If the activities are accomplished, they will produce evidence of service delivery and fidelity of the grant goals (outputs), short- and long-term community changes (outcomes), and long-term systemic changes (broader systemic impacts).

While participants found the model useful, they indicated that the language was not necessarily geared toward indigenous populations. We have worked to re-imagine our work to interject indigenous wisdom and practices. At the Hawaii CLE we were introduced to the concept of Kuleana. Kuleana represents (although we learned that the English language is not fully able to define this term) the ideas and notions of responsibility and the privilege of service. Learning about Kuleana led us to re-imagine the logic model, placing Kuleana at its core.

As a result, we created a new logic model that we called "Planting Your Source in Community." One of the biggest critiques of logic models is that they're too linear and many feel uncomfortable conforming to that linear template. Our new model was more circular, which we felt was appropriate given our conversations on how these different elements of our work really feed each other. And at the core of everything, and feeding all our work, is Kuleana, "the source." Figure 8.1 is the new model groups used to create an action plan for work after the gathering.

Step Three: Gallery Walk

A "Gallery Walk" provides each team with an opportunity to present their plan of action and to receive critical feedback from other teams. One member of each team stays with the team's logic model for action to represent the meaning of the

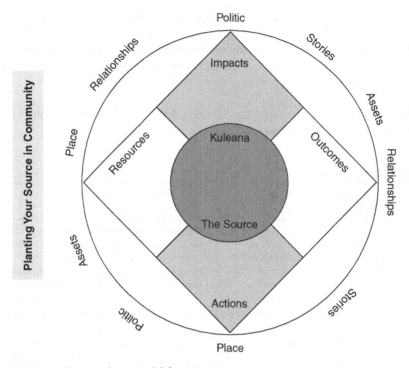

FIGURE 8.1 Indigenous logic model for action

model. Critical friends move from model to model to ask clarifying questions and to post notes on each model.

Step Four: Reflections on Comments

Back in home team, participants look at all suggestions and questions. Have a discussion about what is most helpful to your process and revise your plan based on input from critical friends.

Step Five: Commitment Statements

Make a list of specific commitments from each team member and decide how you will "hold" each other to those commitments.

Logic Model for Action in Action

In Community Learning Exchanges, we use logic model for action to press participants to take action. Putting action steps into writing with measureable, doable outcomes that are publically shared helps in two important ways: (a) it holds teams and team members accountable to implement the actions and (b) it creates a national support structure where others provide input on the plan and can also provide future support networks.

Logic Model for Action Examples

At the Central Texas CLE, members of the North Carolina CLE planning team used this pedagogy to finalize the call for their upcoming CLE. The plan was created with a specific timeline and measurable outcomes. The plan was shared with others at the CLE, and participants provided feedback. Accountability was created as critical friend teams were formed for follow-up after the CLE was concluded.

References and Further Readings

Block, P. (2009). *Community: The structure of belonging.* San Francisco, CA: Berrett-Koehler.

Dewey, J. (1963). *Experience and education.* New York: Collier Books.

Freire, P. (1997). *Pedagogy of the oppressed.* New York: Continuum.

Lundby, K. (2008). Introduction: Digital storytelling, mediatized stories. In K. Lundby (Ed.), *Digital storytelling, mediatized stories: Self representations in new media* (pp. 1–17). New York, NY: Peter Lang.

McKnight, J., & Block, P. (2010). *The abundant community: Awakening the power of families and neighborhoods.* San Francisco, CA: Berrett-Koehler.

Militello, M., & Friend, J. (Eds.). (2013). *Principal 2.0: Technology and educational leadership.* Charlotte, NC: Information Age.

Militello, M., & Guajardo, F. (2013). Virtually speaking: How digital storytelling can facilitate organizational learning. *Journal of Community Positive Practices, 13*(2), 80–91.

Putnam, R.D. (2000). *Bowling alone: The collapse and revival of American community.* New York, NY: Touchstone.

PART IV

Impacts, Reflections, and an Invitation to Action

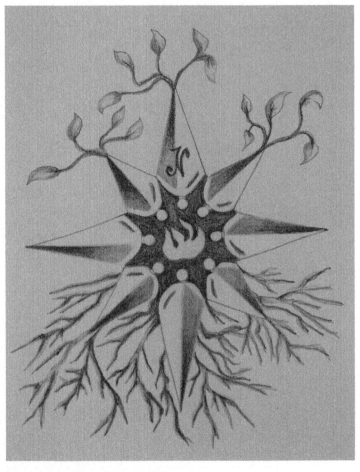

DRAWING 4 Artwork by Mónica Valadez.

Source: Mónica Valadez. Used with permission.

9

IMPACTS FROM AND REFLECTIONS ON THE CLE WORK

CLE Impact

The CLE takes on a number of forms. There is no singular format or template. We have come to realize that the Goldilocks principle (*which one is just right?*) is at play for an effective and meaningful CLE. We have found great success with the three-day and five-day format of our national CLEs, just as we have found success with one-day CLEs that have taken place regionally. There are CLE experiences that happen in even shorter durations (e.g., Dominic's CLE at a funeral) or over a lifetime (e.g., Miguel's children's childhood). Each CLE, formal or informal, long or short has a flow. CLEs embody a commitment to working with others in caring *relationships*, focusing on the *assets* communities possess, telling and listening to *stories*, understanding and honoring *place*, living a *politic* of ethical behavior, and inviting others to take *action*.

Just as there is no one format for a CLE, there are a number of topics or themes that CLEs have focused on (see Appendix A for the list of themes for national CLEs). Being inspired or motivated by the national convening, a number of national participants have gone on to host their own CLEs. For example:

- Larry Hodgkins, a middle school assistant principal, continues to work closely with his university professor, Matt, who introduced him to the CLE work. Matt modeled CLE pedagogies in his principal preparation courses. Additionally, Matt was able to take more than 25 of his master of educational leadership courses to a number of national CLEs over the past five years. Larry was also a member of the North Carolina host team when they hosted a national CLE.

- Subsequently, Larry hosted his own daylong CLE to deeply examine the history of South Creek Middle School in rural northeast North Carolina. Students, teachers, community members, and school board members engaged in RASPPA. South Creek Middle School (SCMS) is an amalgamation of a number of community schools, including segregated schools. SCMS students interacted with community elders who were students of the parent schools of South Creek. The rich, at times traumatic, history was shared and explored. The CLE forged new relationships with community members and the school. School board members wanted to host CLEs at other schools, and the SCMS principal made a commitment to work more closely with community members. The CLE impact was felt at many levels: Individuals became knowledgeable about the history of their community and the organization, and the community was enriched as a result of more people knowing one another's aspirations, desires, and stories.
- Chris and one of his main CLE partners, Sophie Maxis, have worked to reframe traditional "parent information nights" in Jacksonville, Florida. In a series of CLEs they call "The Family Wisdom Exchanges," they have shifted the paradigm from passive disseminations of college admissions data, information, and facts to an actively engaged process designed to position students and family members in their rightful and most effective spaces and roles as the true wisdom and knowledge holders of *their* college-going processes. These Family Wisdom Exchanges quickly transcended the college-going process by becoming a Gracious Space in which students and their families have been able to explore, challenge, and improve other areas of their lives including school policies, processes, and family and community challenges.
  - The Family Wisdom Exchange represents a new narrative about family engagement. It is notable that these Family Wisdom Exchanges have been held within urban community high schools that in some cases have been burdened with uninformed and damaging narratives held by many in the broader community surrounding these neighborhoods. These deficit narratives hold that the parents, caregivers, and family members of the students in these schools are lacking in commitment and motivation to be involved in their students' education and schools. Initially, based on the attendance of their previous parent information nights, district staff members expressed little hope and great pessimism regarding the likely turnout for these Family Wisdom Exchanges. Cynically, they would often say that the only motivation for attendance was the provision of a dinner as part of the gatherings. However, as families actively experienced these exchanges, they were able to bring their own gifts, talents, and wisdom for the benefit of others in their neighborhoods while simultaneously benefiting from others. Attendance increased rapidly, as did enthusiasm. It wasn't long before students and families began identifying the topics of the proceeding exchanges as well as designing and facilitating the exchanges with the planning team.

- Miguel helped steward the energy of a diverse team of educators, graduate and undergraduate students, community partners including a local museum, and professors from his institution to host a national CLE focusing on *The Politics of Education and Community Development: Creating Healthy Communities through Collective Leadership.* Twelve teams from eight states joined the San Marcos, Texas, team to discuss, share, and explore the role of politics in how institutions educate and guide youth. Dynamic conversation, coupled with field trips where participants were able to experience policies in practice, shaped the CLE that culminated in a five-hour session at the state capital, where teams discussed and imagined their work back home. The state capitol building in Austin became a place of the people; the issue at hand was creating the future of the CLE work and addressing the topic at hand. The building became a democratic space for that afternoon. This national CLE event also gave birth to ideas, action plans, and an energy the host team has kept alive in years following the CLE they hosted. The Central Texas team has sustained the rhythm of hosting local and regional CLEs for the purpose of school and community leadership development with multiple stakeholders. The Central Texas team has hosted CLEs annually where they explore youth and adult partnerships for the purpose of community change; they have taught graduate courses utilizing CLE pedagogies with the community being their classroom. They have also utilized CLE pedagogies for leadership development of school district leaders and have facilitated CLEs for university staff and departments as they look to create and build community with their working teams.
  - Miguel's CLE work has informed the teaching, learning, leading, and research methods of his students and their community partners. The dynamic-critical pedagogies have transformed the engaged-methodologies employed in their dissertation research, and the place-based curriculum has informed the development of residents' hall advisors on the university campus, educational leaders, and teachers working with parents and community partners in schools based on their assets, gifts, and visions.
- Francisco teaches and engages in community work through the use of CLE practices and pedagogies. As the chairman of a community action group in his South Texas hometown, he used a CLE to bring more than a dozen community members together to mount a campaign to build new schools in Edinburg, Texas. Using reflective pedagogies à la CLE, the community group worked for a year to establish trust within the group and then set out to engage in a public information campaign to convince the community to vote in favor of a $112 million bond to build new schools. The CLE process worked, and the Edinburg school district has expanded its educational opportunities for local children by building four new elementary schools, two middle schools, and four fine arts centers, and by renovating a high school. Francisco and others have parlayed that experience and used it to effectively advocate to pass another bond issue to improve the drainage infrastructure

countywide. The South Texas county of Hidalgo has since passed a $184 million bond to improve drainage, especially in areas where the most vulnerable people in the region are affected.

• In South Texas, CLEs have changed the nature of university teaching, as these approaches give new definition to what it means to acquire and achieve a higher education. The new approaches bring new players into the work, as CLE redefines the nature of research, service, and teaching by bringing faculty, students, and community members into the work together.

We experienced CLEs in schools, communities, and work settings. What matters most is not the format, but the engagement of a meaningful representation of people around an important topic that needs to be understood and then acted upon for the public good.

Reflections

Taking time to reflect is important, but often ignored in education and community development work. In what follows, we reflect on the work together organizing and facilitating CLEs across the country. We begin by reflecting on the process of trying to put the spirit of the CLE into text. We then reflect on lessons learned at the three ecologies of knowing: self, organization, and community.

The Difficulties of Written Text

We came together for a writing retreat confident that each of us had crafted specific pieces for the book. We would meet, cut and paste some chapters together, and then do a quick read of each other's work and be done.

Our work together began with catching up on stories of our work and families back home. This led us to the need to *see* and *hear* the book's story. We covered the walls of the writing room with rolls of construction paper. As we plastered the story or stories we wanted to tell on the walls, we realized the writing we had was important but incomplete. We had to follow the CLE process; we told the stories, we analyzed and critiqued the stories, and we retold the stories and, subsequently, constructed an action. We re-authored our story as we wove our personal, organizational, and community narrative. We had several Circles and recorded many of our conversations. The conversations seemed to revolve around specific stories of the CLE at work in our local communities and the impacts we witnessed as a result of the work. We did it the CLE way!

These stories fundamentally changed what we wrote. The spaces between writing became the fodder and motivation for the writing; it allowed us to share stories and to identify what needed to be told in the book. As we told stories, someone would say, "That is what you need to write about!" We were reinforcing the notion that we must share the important work we all do. While we do the work, we may not always realize the importance of the work. The CLE-inspired work created a different way we did our own work by breaking traditions and motivating us to make these new traditions the new norm in processes like writing. In the following, we provide an account of the stories we shared with one another. The stories are about *self*, *organizations*, and *communities*. These are our ecologies of knowing. These are our stories.

Self

Matt: I am a voracious reader of fiction. I find reading fiction helps me think, it helps me write, even academic writing! A few summers ago, I decided to read Miguel De Cervantes's *Don Quixote*. It truly is one of the most comical stories ever written. There were only a handful of lines I underscored in the 900 page plus book. This line is stated by Quixote to his squire, Sancho Panza: "*You must look at who you are and make an effort to know yourself, which is the most difficult knowledge one can imagine.*"

PHOTO 9.1 Matt's family and dissertation co-chairs Maenette Benham and Gary Sykes, 2004. Photographer: Susan Damm-Fultz.

I am a different person because of my involvement in the Community Learning Exchange work. The pedagogies we work with and the relationships that have evolved have transformed me. They did so by helping me make an effort to know myself.

My mentor introduced me to this work in my PhD program. Dr. Maenette Benham opened a new world to me. She helped liberate my traditional understandings of research and evaluation. She taught me the importance of working with site elders and youth. She modeled the graciousness and relationship building that should be prerequisites for human interactions in any walk of life. But Maenette was savvy to understand that these ideals needed to be lived in communities that are marginalized and in communities that have experiences with "outside experts" and strict hierarchical models of leadership. Together, we engaged in powerful, mutual learning experiences across the country. Each visit, each site, amplified my learning and my growth. This is the learning that has shaped me—even more than the formal university degrees. My direct work with people like Maenette and my interactions with community members across the country have helped me understand what is meant by *community as text*.

Because of this work, I am a different teacher, researcher, father, son, and husband. I teach in a very different way (yes, in Circles, not rows). I conduct research with a very different focus (engaging *with* participants), and I engage with my family and community through a very different lens, not as a fixer but as a listener of story to engage in dialogue that generates local solutions. The turning point for me was digging into my own story. Quixote may have been on a fool's errand and may have been seen as an idiot by many, but he was one knight errant who at least understood the difficulty and importance of knowing one's self.

Miguel and Francisco Guajardo: We came to this country the last day of the year in 1968. Our parents made a bold move that would chart the rest our lives. They left their land, a modest home, and their relatives in search of a better life for their children—that was their dream. Historians write that this was the year that changed the world; it certainly was a year that changed our lives. Our parents modeled bold actions, and we have lived with the understanding that life requires these types of bold moves, ideas, and moments of faith. Our parents set the example for who we were as Mexicanos and who we could become as border crossers. They did not know the specifics, but they taught us the need to be well educated, or *ser bién educados*. Our father had a fourth grade education in rural Mexico; our mother did not attend any formal schooling. Both graduated from what our father pegged in his autobiography as *"La Universidad de la Vida"* (The University of Life). They both modeled critical thinking, how to be socially responsible citizens, and, perhaps more importantly, how to *procurar la familia y las amistades* (how to be good to family and friends). They were our intellectual and moral lodestar. Our personal and professional identities are a direct consequence of our parents' influence.

Our parents also learned from our *abuelitos* (grandparents) the cycle of life and the need to pay it forward. Our father frequently quoted his mother, our *abuela* Virginia: "*Mi'jo, dale la mano a gente con necesidad, porque ayer fui yo, hoy son ellos y mañana serán mis hijos*" (Son, give a helping hand to those in need, because yesterday it was me, today it is them, and tomorrow it will be my children).

We have had the privilege to travel around the world and had experiences that persistently piqued our parents' curiosity. They often asked about how other people lived and how their cultures were expressed; they asked about plants, animals, and climates. We brought pictures, videos, and stories and even brought some of our new friends from other parts of the world with us. Our parents learned from our travels and from our work. The world became their playground as they lived vicariously through us. Our parents never spoke nor wrote English, but they were very literate people. They taught us the art of conversation, the science of questioning, and the willingness to ask insightful questions as they nurtured our curiosity. Our mother is wont to say "*con cariño, casi todo se puede preguntar*" (with love and tenderness, you can ask just about any question). They were curious about life and society and inspired similar behaviors in us. They understood they had a responsibility to give back to our community, and they gave habitually—this was a great gift they bestowed upon us. But it was more than a symbolic gift, because they expected this behavior from us. So we have become public educators, community builders, and activists.

Chris: The experience of my first national CLE in Washington, DC, inspired and provoked personal growth. There I first witnessed and experienced expressions of collective leadership and learning so full it was contagious. It was beyond any pedagogy I had known; it felt dynamic. As a teacher and counselor, relationships were central to how I worked, but there I began to recognize how the institutions that were so prominent in my life—public schools, the academy, and the professional academic organizations for those working within them—were functioning to compartmentalize my relationships. In allowing this compartmentalization, I had permitted my life to become fragmented and disconnected. I saw other professors being in relationship with participants in authentic and whole ways. I listened to Francisco and Miguel share stories about their father. I watched Miguel and Matt coach and encourage each other's sons, Emiliano and Dominic, on how to engage other participants in conversations that might encourage their development. People learned together, laughed together, cried together, and planned together. There was an energy to the experience that stayed with me.

On the plane back to Jacksonville, I realized some central absurdities. I knew about collective leadership in an intellectual, academic way, but I was not practicing it fully enough in my work at the university, and I was not living it fully enough in my personal life. While I was teaching graduate students about the virtues of collective leadership, my pedagogy did not always reflect its values; the curriculum I was using was drawn excessively from published scholarship, leaving insufficient space for the curriculum of students' experiences, lives, and stories. The boundaries between my life and my work were unnecessarily rigid. I now knew that it did not have to be that way. I had seen examples that were very different from that institutionalized separation and those institutionalized relationships. Those different examples exuded great authenticity and genuineness. Among these examples was the therapeutic impact I saw Francisco's personal stories have on others; the fatherly, supportive, and challenging conversations I overheard Miguel having with youth; and the way Matt used his gift of humor to add needed levity following emotionally trying conversations. Collectively, these examples and many more formed a new story of professors in community, of activist scholars. It was not only a new story of integrated and whole lives but also one of greater effectiveness and impact in giving others opportunities to lead within their own schools and communities.

The CLEs also helped me address the incongruence between my value of community in the abstract and the concrete reality that my family and I did not know any of our neighbors of two years. This lack of community was impacting my two young sons Dylan and Jack. They would often look out the window into our cul-de-sac and observe the three similar-aged children two houses down and report to us, "The kids are out playing again." Two years and two houses down and we had not yet learned the names of these neighbors, or any neighbors, for that matter. I knew that had to change. After sharing with my wife, Mary Beth, what I had experienced and learned at the CLE, we resolved that we could and should change things in our home and our neighborhood. We began by going door to door and reintroducing ourselves to our neighbors, reengaging with them, and together re-envisioning what our neighborhood could become. We learned our neighbors' names, and we began building relationships together. We discovered that our neighbors also felt the isolation our family did. We were amused to find out that the children our sons referred to as "the kids" referred to our sons as "the boys" while they had also watched them from their window.

It took surprisingly little time to turn things around in our cul-de-sac from our private isolation to a public community. Our experience brought to life some important principles of systems and how they can be impacted. Small actions led to big changes. For example, during our first reintroduction conversation with our next-door neighbors, they responded enthusiastically with the idea that our cul-de-sac represented a great and safe space for our children to play and grow together. He mentioned that in his backyard was an old, portable basketball hoop lying in disrepair. He offered to repair, restore, and place it out in the street. It was a hit with our kids. That hoop became the center of their play, and when they tired of basketball in the Florida sun, they arranged folding chairs at the end of our driveways to talk and share like people once did on front porches or storefronts. That hoop also began to attract more kids from down the street and from the neighborhoods around us. And with them came their parents. Soon our evenings and weekends consisted of children and families talking, playing, and building friendships.

Years have passed now and our families and children have grown—many stretching the limits of the space in our homes. Yet no one leaves. There is a collective understanding that something special has occurred. We recognize that our relationships are more important than roomier houses. I know my sons would never let us move. They have grown through their friendships with our neighbors and we have as well. I also know that my family now understands that they can change their communities through building relationships. They have experienced the gifts that accompany the belief that they have the power to build relationships with others and the belief that those relationships can nurture their growth, meet their needs, and bring the joys that accompany great friendships. I owe a lot of those gifts to things I have learned in CLEs.

Organization

Francisco and Miguel: Organizations have multiple roles in our society. We have learned from studying modern organizations (including schools, religious institutions, and families) that these very organizations can be forces for social control, vehicles to provide order in society, or engines to liberate the human mind and spirit. Unfortunately for those of us who are introduced to public schools in the United States, we learn quickly that there is little room for creativity, original thought, or democratic living. In *Schooling in Capitalist America*, Bowles and Gintis (1976) pose the question: "How can our initial introduction into formal organizations in a democratic society be so undemocratic?" We acknowledge this condition, but we also elect to change it. Within these normative structures we learned how to be organizational public people. We were taught at home that the professionals in schools were the most important people in the community, and we believed this story. We believed it so much so that we wanted to be important people in the community, so we became teachers. Our story took a significant turn because we experienced spaces in schools where teaching and mentoring provoked our curiosity and imagination. We found opportunities to imagine different ways of thinking, different ways of teaching and learning, and different ways of engaging in community life.

Schools were never separated from our home. They worked in tandem to make sure we received the education we needed to be effective citizens in a democratic society. Our parents were in constant conversation with teachers, principals, and other school personnel. Within the public school we found the necessary opportunities to become the public educators of our parents' dreams. We found academic mentors such as Marta Longoria, Henry Trueba, Pedro Reyes, Jay Scribner Sr., Jim Scheurich, Maenette Benham, Doug Foley, and numerous others who nurtured us and saw the value in the educational and community development ideas we lived and worked by in the community. In higher education, our mentors invited us to come into the academy and study the academic side of the work. These conversations have engendered interest in certain sectors of the academy, because the work has relevancy to the modern context. It is work that responds to the critical issues of the day, what Gary Orfield called in his 2014 Brown AERA Lecture "a new civil rights agenda for American Education." Beyond the policy research and advocacy work, we believe academics should also help schools and other public institutions engage in a re-culturalization process. If not, they may soon experience their own demise, as they may cease to be relevant to communities in which they exist.

Matt and Chris: Our friendship began when we worked together in a high school in Michigan—Matt as an assistant principal and Chris as a school counselor. It was through our work together with kids that we recognized we were kindred spirits. We fought the establishment and the traditions of the school and the community to address issues of race (minority students sent to the alternative school) and equity (supporting the establishment of a GLBT group in a very conservative community). Together we also experienced vivid examples of how organizations, and some of the people in them, attempt to resist, undermine, and confront those who seek to change and reform them. Our time in that high school ended when we each left to enter PhD programs in different states, but our work together continued.

We quickly discovered that universities were also places in which old conventions and methods served to limit needed innovation. Most produced in our universities and the colleges of education is very traditional in both design and practice. We both found these traditional approaches and methods of doing research to be inhibiting and constrictive. Previously we had focused our work in public schools on helping youth find ways to empower themselves and make their voices heard. Now that we were in the academy, it was difficult to see how most of the research conducted around us could serve to empower anyone. In fact, participants are often marginalized by positioning them as merely data points or passive informants. Our shared sense of restriction and discomfort within the research traditions of the academy provoked our spirits to explore different approaches to learning with people in ways that honored their perspectives. In the process of that exploration we had the good fortune to learn about a relatively unknown, and misunderstood, research approach called Q methodology from one of its masters, Steve Brown, at the institution where Chris was earning his PhD.

Q methodology spoke (and still speaks) to us on a number of levels. It honors the perspectives of participants in substantive ways throughout the research process; it is nuanced, complex, and imaginative; and it is understood by many of its practitioners to be subject to marginalization itself by those who struggle to recognize its ingenuity and other gifts. Together, we spent a great deal of time learning and engaging in Q methodology and began to stretch its uses even beyond its community of passionate practitioners. We soon began applying it to our evaluation projects. But it was not until we brought Q methodology into the CLE that true transformation occurred—for our evaluation work, for the CLEs, and for the methodology as well.

The CLE focus on relationships helped us think about how we could push that element of the methodology beyond the statistical relationships. We had the willingness to imagine that we could extend the participatory nature of the methodology even further than developing the research instrument and collecting participant data. We could, and should, strive to empower participants to analyze and make meaning from their own data. In doing so, we have pushed our own research and evaluation work to completely new places. Developing a hybrid research and evaluation methodology focused on relationships and the power of place and wisdom of local people creates a deep participatory foundation to research that is fundamentally different from what we were taught and told to do. It is no longer simply Q methodology. It is an investigation, an exploration, an InQuiry, which participants engage in together around their individual, shared, and collective perspectives. In recognition of this transformed use and purpose, the language we use has changed. We call the perspectives shared by participants "families" rather than statistical factors.

PHOTO 9.2 InQuiry in action, Hawaii. Photographer: Matthew Militello.

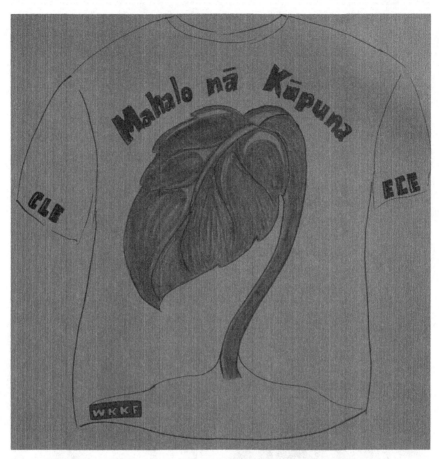

PHOTO 9.3 Participant's analysis through the InQuiry process. Photographer: Matthew Militello.

We also invite participants to be involved in the analysis through their own languages, their own cultural and community contexts, and their own gifts. InQuiry has taught us that our roles as evaluators need not be limited to the conventions of the field and profession (see more about InQuiry in the *Dynamic-Critical Pedagogies* section). Yes, we measure and assess, but we do it alongside people in communities who are striving to improve schools and other organizations so they better support the lives and development of their youth and families.

In the end, we have integrated our evaluation and research work with our CLE lives and communities. We also now think about research very differently—we have a new awareness. The CLE axioms and theory of change (RASPPA) are now lived through our research and evaluation. We did not learn this through the traditional university coursework, rather through the relationships and mentoring that occurs through the CLE. This work has equipped us to re-culture our own universities in spaces that are ready for dynamic-critical pedagogies.

Community

Matt: This work has pushed me to build community. As a faculty member at North Carolina State University, I was a co-director of a multi-million-dollar, federally funded Race to the Top (RttT) grant. This grant was geared to support the preparation of future school leaders in a rural part of North Carolina. The Northeast Leadership Academy (NELA) was formed, and three cohorts of educators received full scholarships with the promise of a different model of preparation.

The scope and sequence for a new, innovative preparation needed to be rooted in more than just a full scholarship and a full-time internship. What I brought to NELA were the Community Learning Exchange (CLE) axioms, theory of change (RASPPA), and dynamic-critical pedagogies. I want to highlight three specific CLE elements that became an instrumental part of the preparation program: community engagement, storytelling, and leading local CLEs.

An important part of the preparation became an intense, summer-long community internship. NELA Fellows worked in a community-based organization as part of a six-credit course. Dr. Doris Williams, executive director of the *Rural School and Community Trust*, taught the course; we purposely found a community-based advocate to lead this course. Community internships are not the norm in school leadership preparation, but they do exist. The NELA Fellows engaged in an internship experience that focused on depth, not breadth. Fellows spent their 16 weeks immersed in community life, engaging *in* and *with* community. The summer learning experience was rooted with the community as the textbook and the assignments.

The cohorts were introduced to this new kind of preparation with a Digital Storytelling retreat. Each year, at least five members of the national CLE team spent two days with the NELA Fellows to participate in a process of self-examination, leadership, and Digital Storytelling. Fellows engaged in the pedagogies of Circle, Learning Walks, World Café, Meaningful Conversations, and Play. The pedagogies were utilized to push the Fellows to think about who they were as emerging leaders, and who and what shaped them. The stories that emerged were powerful expressions of self and were shared with the NELA community in a public setting. In the end, the stories impacted individuals as well as the group at large (see *Video Links* for digital stories).

What I am most proud of, most impressed by, most inspired by, is the fact that so many NELA Fellows are practicing CLE axioms, theory of change, and

PHOTO 9.4 Students at a digital Storytelling retreat. Photographer: Matthew Militello.

dynamic-critical pedagogies. The RttT grant afforded me the opportunity to take Fellows to CLEs across the country: in places such as South Texas, Central Texas, New York, Tennessee, Montana, Florida, Washington, and the District of Columbia. Fellows practiced the CLE work in the NELA courses and with national audiences. The result of the steady diet of CLE spirit and dynamic-critical pedagogies was that they began to live the work. Fellows planned and implemented their own CLE pedagogies as well as local CLEs.

The NELA graduate community is a community of practice, a community where participants network and live the work they find so important to their development. For school leaders, community-engaged work is inspiring and humbling. Moreover, as their mentor, I am similarly humbled to see the Fellows engaging in community building, digital storytelling, and implementing local CLEs. The Fellows are paying the CLE spirit and work forward.

Chris: I think about the different ways that we have brought the work of the CLEs back to Jacksonville, the University of North Florida, and to the local school district. We have held numerous daylong CLEs, and elements of the CLE axioms, social technologies, and pedagogies have become embedded more and more into the practices of schools, churches, and other organizations.

As much as it has spread into these various places, the relationships within our local team have changed. For example, when Keon Whaley is on campus, he will stop by to check in, and we will talk about our families as well as our community work. Rudy Jamison and I will go out to lunch and share stories along with strategies for navigating our organizations. Natalie Medina and her children will stop by my house. When Sophie is in, we will work out of the same office. One way we have stayed committed to the spirit, axioms, and principles of our shared work is to frame our collective as family. We discuss how the perspective that we are a family helps us to help one another mediate all of our different obligations, responsibilities, and opportunities within the organizations that pay us or grant us degrees. We also think and plan strategically regarding how we are going to take care of each other. This means that we are invested in each other's development and that this investment needs to be expressed through planned action. It is this new frame of family that has moved and impacted others who have encountered our work to take some of this spirit of family back to their own organizations. We have found that many, if not most, desire to work within communities that support and nurture us as we experience within our families.

The other impact the CLE has had on our Jacksonville community has grown from our emphasis on community narratives, in particular, those narratives that have become hidden or otherwise ignored but that represent key examples of people here working together to bring about change. These key stories have been from the present and from the past. For example, Murray Hill Christ Community Church could very well go unnoticed among the larger pool of churches in this dense region of the Bible belt. However, as described previously, the work of the Murray Hill Christ Community Church congregation and leadership team *should be elevated*. Its story should be told. Murray Hill may be small (particularly compared to some of the mega-churches in the area), but their spirit of collective leadership is profound, their impact is great, and their story should be known so others can learn from it.

The story of Murray Hill has not been told up until now due to its size, position, and modesty, but there are other stories in Jacksonville that are not told because they are dangerous. The story of the 1960 lunch counter sit-ins in downtown Jacksonville and the subsequent White racist response called "Ax Handle Saturday" is one of those stories. In the view of our local CLE team, the story of the sit-ins represents the most significant social progress that has occurred in Jacksonville over the past 100 years. Incredibly, high school students and a high school teacher led these sit-ins, yet many of our residents, even the deeply rooted ones, are unaware of it. Thus, this story became the central narrative of our national CLE themed around "Moral Courage." Even more, it was told during our CLE by the man who led those sit-ins as the then 16-year-old president of the Youth Council of the Jacksonville NAACP, our community elder and teacher, Rodney Hurst.

It was Rodney's words spoken to me recently that have stayed with me. Rodney told me that because of the work we are doing in Jacksonville, we should be careful. He said to me in an almost whispered tone that the CLE work we are engaging in, that the relationships we are having, the people we are having them with, and the stories we are telling are dangerous. He explained that our efforts to create spaces and processes, in and through which people might empower themselves through telling their stories, are very scary to many people in this community, so we need to watch out for ourselves. His words startled me. After all, we are talking about relationships and stories. It made me think about the idea that if you engage in truly transformational change, then you will receive pushback in some serious and significant ways. To me, that speaks to the power of relationships and stories; the power to change things is so profound that those relationships and stories are perceived as a threat to those invested in maintaining the status quo.

I see the impact of our relationships and use of stories here in Jacksonville when they are used for developmental purposes. People are resonating with these dynamic-critical pedagogies. These stories are powerful to people here, and their power transcends any specific narrative that it is our responsibility as citizens to contribute to the re-authoring of Jacksonville. The fact that people here need a space where someone purposefully invites them in to tell their stories also means that we have work to do because they should not require an external invitation. We hope this aspect will grow in our community. At the same time, it forces a recognition that Rodney had and shared with me—a recognition that true, authentic relationships and storytelling are radical acts, especially to those within institutions that do not wish to share their power and control. That makes the work of the CLE all the more important and all the more necessary.

Francisco and Miguel: Our eldest brother Pepe continued the legacy of service our parents taught us. Pepe graduated at the top of his high school class and could have selected any profession and university to attend, but he wanted to be a teacher and thus set the trajectory for the rest of us. We all followed his example. At the ripe age of 21, Pepe went back to our high school to become a teacher, a job he committed to for the next 30 years. He taught us commitment to place and to profession.

Pepe taught us how to read, write, and imagine. We also learned from him that our work had to come back home, and so for the last 25 years, we too have done our work in the place we call home. We formalized the Llano Grande work in the community that raised us and in the high school where we learned how to appreciate community. The school hallways are where we made friends and where we learned about school pride, how to lead, and how to have fun. Living in federal housing, we learned how to organize teams, build baseball and football fields, and create games with old tire rims or a 10 cent ball and a broken broomstick, among other things. This is the community that allowed us to take risks as teenage leaders, and then as young quixotic teachers who believed the world was our laboratory for teaching, learning, and expanding our imagination. The community ensured we exercised the permission to dream and nurtured an intellectual and cultural renaissance in our own little part of the world, rural South Texas.

Our college preparation and youth community development programs catapulted our small community to national recognition and has gifted us a space to stand on. Archimedes' spatial wisdom offers an axiom, where we make sense of our hometown as a place to stand, where we can move the world. Just as our move to this country changed our world, this community nurtured in us a spirit of change that we take seriously and use to move the world of young people and parents. We stand on the strength of this rural community and its people, and the CLE and other community engagement pedagogies have been our lever and fulcrum as we work to move the world to a better place.

Meta-Reflection

Stories help us understand and translate the work of the CLEs. The stories push this book to a space beyond a how-to treatise and allow us to take you into a deeper level of the CLE experience. We want to show—as best we can in a book—what takes place, how it takes place, and the impact the work has. We want to model the important use of story, because stories bring learning, relationships, and community to life. We invite you to reflect on the gifts that you bring to yourself, your organization, and your community. What's *your* story?

PHOTO 9.5 The authors, Miguel, Matt, Chris, and Francisco, writing at the Cedarbrake Retreat Center in Belton, Texas. Photographer: The authors.

References and Further Readings

Bowles, S., & Gintis, H. (1976). *Schooling in a capitalistic America: Educational reform and the contradictions of economic life*. New York, NY: Basic Books.

Guajardo, J.A. (1986). *Anécdotas de la vida de José Angel Guajardo: Por insistencia de Francisco Guajardo*. Unpublished manuscript.

Orfield, G. (2014). Tenth Annual Brown Lecture in Education Research: A new civil rights agenda for American education. *American Educational Research Journal, 43*(6), 273–292.

10

CONCLUSION AND AN INVITATION TO ACTION

The Community Learning Exchange moves the mind and the spirit. It is cognitive, affective, and dynamic. It is a healing process. Whatever brings participants to the work, whatever the experience they have at the exchange, the feedback consistently points to deep transformation. Moving experiences should not be relegated to special events or within the confines of family. Communities—where one lives and works—should be host to moving experiences. Community Learning Exchanges provide the spaces and dynamic-critical pedagogies to move people, organizations, and communities to better places.

At the beginning of the book we ask readers to consider a set of questions. We invite you to revisit these questions as a challenge to move from understanding to application.

* What stories do you need to explore about yourself, your organization, and your community?
* Who do you need to talk with to reflect on this book?
* Who else needs to read this book?
* What is your plan of action, including the principles (axioms), theory of change (RASPPA), and strategies (dynamic-critical pedagogies)?

The CLE finds inspiration and follows the work of a number of organizing and social change models, including the historic work of the Highlander Center in Tennessee. The respect Highlander paid working class people and everyday citizens is instructive to the approach of the CLE. We borrow from Highlander's mantra that suggests, "The answers to the problems facing society lie in the experiences of ordinary people." We hope that we convey this message and demonstrate how this work can impact people, organizations, and communities. The interactive and authentic acts of pedagogy when paired with the ecologies of knowing and that can help us reimagine teaching and learning in our communities, as we create a place and space for the development of a new way of knowing.

Community Learning Exchanges can take many forms and can have many functions. Regardless of its shape and regardless of the intended outcomes, they are anchored by the axioms, theory of change (RASPPA), and dynamic-critical pedagogies chronicled in this book. We have illustrated what a CLE looks like, what it feels like, and how it impacts participants and hosts alike. The experience allows us to re-author our stories in the following ways:

- from alienation and independence to connection and interdependence
- from passivity and reliance to action and agency
- from deficiency and poverty to abundance
- from those who are spoken for to those who speak
- from community issues and problems to community solutions and possibilities
- from a prescriptive system of teaching to a dynamic-critical pedagogy for learning

Communities need positive and healthy ways to move forward. We need to understand and honor the past. We also need to reveal truths in order to craft new narratives owned by and lived by the very people and places that need positive changes.

The work is inspiring, provocative, and, for some, even therapeutic. These words are not often used to describe a conference, a workshop, or an institute. We use the concept of "exchange" purposefully. An exchange honors teaching *and* learning. An exchange empowers everyone to have a voice. An exchange seeks first to understand the spaces and places in community. An exchange builds on the assets a community already has. An exchange is action oriented. An exchange is inquiry minded. An exchange is reflective. An exchange builds meaningful and thoughtful relationships among all attendees. An exchange creates local and national networks of people committed to reframing school and community partnerships. Exchanges evoke and provoke relationships anchored in principles of family, of democracy, and of relationships.

From personal experiences and community conversations with students, community partners, and families, we know people want happy and healthy communities where they can live, work, and raise children. Such communities need social capital—social capital within ourselves, our organizations, and our communities. We present these stories of love for our communities as action for fostering this social capital. The social capital our parents gave each of us are gifts that nurtured our respective abilities to care, to dream, and to develop the skills to act on our own behalf, which in turn has helped us help others figure out ways to act for themselves.

The work is inherently disruptive, because it creates change. Change is difficult. Change has individual, organizational, institutional, and cultural ramifications. *Change comes by design.* The Community Learning Exchange work is our design to create opportunities for change. The work of the CLE bridges theory and practice. It builds relationships that honor the wisdom of our elders and the vitality of our youth; it focuses on assets; and it challenges deficit thinking with a relentless focus on the power of the local.

> This book is a call,
> an invitation to *imagine*,
> a promise of *hope*,
> an opportunity to *think*, and
> a call to *act*!

Reference and Further Readings

Horton, M., & Jacobs, D. (2003). *The Myles Horton reader: Education for social change.* Knoxville, TN: University of Tennessee Press.

APPENDIX

Connecting the Wisdom and Leadership of Place

CLE Title: **Lead on: Igniting Youth Voice and Choice**
Co-Hosted by: **National Collaboration on Workforce and Disability for Youth (NCWD/Youth) and Institute for Educational Leadership (IEL)**
Location: **Washington, DC**
Date: **December 11–14, 2014**

"Lead On" is a phrase commonly used by the disability community when advocating for civil rights issues. Justin Dart, Jr., often known as the father of the Americans with Disabilities Act and the godfather of the disability rights movement, popularized the phrase as a call to action. As a testament to Dart's legacy, and NCWD/Youth's long history of developing youth leaders, the Lead On CLE brought together youth, youth with disabilities, and their peer and adult allies in efforts to increase youth voice. This CLE was organized by IEL and its National Collaboration on Workforce and Disabilities to focus on youth with disabilities and their access to voice and choice as they transition from high school to adulthood. The CLE was hosted at Gallaudet University to represent a historical and current location that serves youth and adults with disabilities. The Kellogg Center Conference Center and the Gallaudet campus offered a varied and deep history of supporting persons who are deaf.

CLE Title: **Peacemaking and Healing: Leadership Practices for Healthy, Inclusive Communities**
Hosted by: **Center for Ethical Leadership**
Location: **Seattle, WA**
Date: **May 15–18, 2014**

Many of us have dedicated our lives to creating healthy, just, and inclusive communities, or what Dr. Martin Luther King Jr. called the *beloved community*. He suggests this community has "a . . . level of relationships among people . . . where justice prevails and persons attain their full human potential." To bring about this community requires leadership that practices a "type of spirit and type of love that can transform opposers into friends."

At this CLE, teams of 3–5 people deeply exploring peacemaking and healing as critical leadership practices. We explored questions such as the following:

* Where in your community do you need peacemaking and healing?
* What does peacemaking and healing look like in your community?
* What would a healthy and inclusive community look like to you?
* What are you willing to do to build your leadership practice of peacemaking and healing?

CLE Title: **Moral Courage: The Heart of Faith, Education, and Change**
Hosted by: **University of North Florida**
Location: **Jacksonville, FL**
Date: **October 9–12, 2014**

As evidenced by the continued challenges to transform our public schools and systems into more equitable and just places to address recent tragedies of violence against young African American men (both in northeast Florida and nationally), the need for moral courage to help support and enact needed changes has never been greater. Participants worked to continue collaborative efforts of local community members and national allies who engage in organizational and community change through the collective leadership.

The Jacksonville–St. Augustine region where the learning exchange was held is a powerful place to explore and develop moral courage. The area is home to powerful stories—both historical and current—that illustrate how moral courage can both fuel and mediate efforts to change communities and the organizations within them through faith and education. These northeast Florida stories were brought to life as a living curriculum and context through which participants engaged with local pioneers of the civil rights movement. Additionally, participants experienced site visits that provided teams with opportunities to reflect and exchange with contemporary activists about the role moral courage plays in their respective approaches for community-led empowerment and change.

CLE Title: **Looking Back to Move Forward: Leading for Racial Healing in Schools, Families, and Communities**
Hosted by: **North Carolina State University**
Location: **Franklinton Center at Bricks, Whitakers, NC**
Date: **October 10–13, 2013**

The first step toward creating change within your community is looking back to understand the past. Then, armed with that knowledge and understanding, you are able to work with others to move forward and build a brighter future.

The theme of looking back in order to move forward guided this CLE. Teams from around the country—from California and Texas to Florida and North Carolina—gathered at the Franklinton Center at Bricks in Whitakers, North Carolina. The Franklinton Center has deep historical significance in this part of the United States, and this location was the foundation for conversations about what the theme "looking back to move forward" truly means.

Each team that participated in the learning exchange included youth and school and community leaders, each of whom brought valuable experiences and perspectives to the weekend:

- School leader (principal, assistant principal, teacher, superintendent)
- Youth (middle or high schooler, or recent high school graduate)
- Community leader/activist
- Additional school/family/community member

CLE Title: **The Art(s) of Leadership: A CLE Focused on Youth Adult Partnerships**
Hosted by: **Texas State University, College of Education**
Location: **San Marcos, TX**
Date: **July 25–28, 2013**

This learning exchange illustrated the importance of youth voices in the collective leadership process. Of the 70 participants, half were under the age of 25.

The youth participating in the CLE worked as teams that included adults to do strategic and policy planning to improve their own communities—whether they were from North Carolina, Maryland, Minnesota, Texas, or somewhere in between.

CLE Title: **Realigning Systems to Support the Well-Being of Families and Children**
Hosted by: **Hawai'inuiakea School of Hawaiian Knowledge, University of Hawaii at Manoa**
Location: **Honolulu, HI**
Date: **June 5–9, 2013**

In partnership with the University of Hawaii's School of Hawaiian Knowledge, this learning exchange focused on reclaiming cultural wisdom as a source of community well-being.

'A 'ohe hana nui ke alo 'ia (No task is too big when done together by all) was the theme of this learning exchange, which we co-hosted with the Engaging Communities in Education initiative. The focus was on reclaiming cultural wisdom as a source of community wellbeing. The goal was to reimagine how systems can align more meaningfully across similar and dissimilar organizations, both in and across local communities and across geographical and philosophical boundaries.

Embedded in native Hawaiian culture for the learning exchange, we used a "go to the source" model to help participants honor their own cultures, histories, spirits, and connections to place, in order to build strong relationships capable of sustaining their communities. Throughout the learning exchange, community teams looked to the roots of culture and language to explore how to create more innovative systems to support and engage families and children. This focus provided a solid foundation upon which to support stronger infrastructure capable of building stronger and healthier families.

An exciting mix of communities participated in this CLE, including: the Salish/Kootenai, Lummi, Seneca, White Clay, Acoma, and Laguna tribal nations; the National Rites of Passage; Llano Grande Center; and groups from across the Hawaiian islands (Ka Honua Momona, Aha Punana Leo, Kauhale o Waini'anae, INPEACE, and Kamehameha Schools).

CLE Title: **Reclaiming Education as a Tool for Healing**
Hosted by: **Salish Kootenai College**
Location: **Pablo, MT**
Date: **August 16–19, 2012**

This learning exchange explored the roots of the traumatic relationship between the Salish, Kootenai, and Pend d'Oreille people and Western education and provided opportunities to share how Indian communities and tribes are now reclaiming education as a tool for healing and leadership within their communities. Over three days, many people shared stories of how they have started to rebuild both the education system and their culture. Participants also spent time planning action steps to bring home with them to reclaim the education systems in their own communities to bring more healing and hope.

Education has always been a part of the lives of the Salish, Kootenai, and Pend d'Oreille people. Traditionally, knowledge was passed from generation to generation in order to teach the skills and beliefs needed for life. Most of this knowledge was transmitted through oral traditions in individual homes and communities, until the introduction of non-Native educational practices and institutions. The power of education to influence and shape one's culture—one's identity—was recognized by the church and state, and was employed as a tool for destroying traditional Native life. The purpose of the assimilative educational practices was to destroy Native identities, including languages, traditions, and families, and has resulted in historical trauma and collective grief passed from one generation to the next within our communities.

CLE Title: Teach While Learning/Learn While Teaching
Hosted by: P.S. 24 Brooklyn
Location: Brooklyn, NY
Date: June 7–10, 2012

This learning exchange centered on the idea that teaching and learning are profoundly connected and enhance one another. Participants explored the Sunset Park neighborhood in Brooklyn, a vibrant, densely populated immigrant neighborhood on the Brooklyn waterfront. They also visited dual-language immersion and single-language classrooms, told personal stories, and listened to the stories of others in order to understand the power that all members of a school community can cultivate as they teach while learning and learn while teaching.

CLE Title: The Politics of Education and Community Development: Creating Healthy Communities Through Collective Leadership
Hosted by: Texas State University at San Marcos
Location: San Marcos, TX
Date: January 5–8, 2012

In this learning exchange, 12 teams from eight states came together to work on their local issues in education and community development. As community teams walked the Texas State University campus and visited the statue of a young Lyndon Johnson, they shared their stories and the experiences of their communities. Just as President Johnson used his stories to shape future actions, the CLE teams imagined what they could do in their communities. To reinforce the idea that public institutions exist for the people of a community, we held action-planning sessions in meeting rooms at the state capitol in nearby Austin. At each step of the learning exchange process, the context supported the work of these teams.

> *CLE Title*: **The Role of Public Education in Our Society: What Is the Narrative That We Create Going Forward?**
> *Co-Hosted by*: **The Community Learning Exchange and Journalism That Matters**
> *Location*: **Highlander Institute, TN**
> *Date*: **September 22–25, 2011**

The Community Learning Exchange convened a thought leader meeting on September 22–25, 2011, at the Highlander Center outside of Knoxville, Tennessee. Invitees represented multiple entry points into issues of public education, community-based leadership development, youth voice, social justice, and journalism.

The theme for this gathering looked at the role of public education in society: *What is our narrative of education going forward? How do we tell that story? How do our stories add up? What is the action going forward?* This CLE offered participants an opportunity to reflect and think together, learn more about each other, and deepen partnerships. Participants also explored common ground around messaging and promoting a narrative of education that serves us all well, informs and educates our various constituencies, and counters the dominant narrative around education reform. The dialogue centered on questions such as the following:

- How can we become proactive rather than reactive to forces trying to destroy public education?
- What is the story of education that elevates voices from inside the system? From community?
- What does it mean for education to be the next civil rights issue?
- What will these educational issues look like in 10, 20, or 50 years? Where are we heading? What are we building? What kind of society are we creating, and what's the role of education in creating that society?

> *CLE Title*: **Weaving Strong Communities: Forming Collective Leadership to Advance Just and Equitable Communities**
> *Hosted by*: **Center for Ethical Leadership**
> *Location*: **Seattle, WA**
> *Date*: **May 19–22, 2011**

The Community Learning Exchange (CLE) convened in Seattle, Washington, and guided participants in the formation and use of collective leadership to develop deeper partnerships, broaden community dialogue and engagement, and plan concrete next steps to advance local social change initiatives. The gathering offered lessons from the new *Collective Leadership Storybook: Weaving Strong Communities*, written by members of the CLE network. The 60 participants came from 14 different states and Puerto Rico, and represented 12 different teams or community organizations.

CLE Title: **National Youth Summit**
Hosted by: **U.S. Department of Education**
Location: **Washington, DC**
Date: **February 24–26, 2011**

The backdrop for this learning exchange was the Voices in Action National Youth Summit (see http://www.ed.gov/college-completion/youth-summit#desc). "Voices in Action" was the culminating event of a yearlong listening tour by the Department of Education, designed to learn, from students, ways to increase the college completion rate in the United States. Our CLE network brought high school and college-age students from five states to be part of the summit and share lessons of storytelling and collective leadership as practices that are working in our communities to improve high school graduation and college completion rates. Of the 400 plus people at the Voices in Action National Youth Day Summit, the only Native American and Native Hawaiian representatives were from the CLE network.

CLE Title: **Youth, Families, and Immigration Reform**
Hosted by: **Augustana Lutheran Church, in partnership with Roca, Inc.**
Location: **Washington, DC**
Date: **July 14–17, 2010**

Participants in this timely CLE exchanged knowledge and practices that support family cohesion in an increasingly hostile, anti-immigrant environment. For participating institutions and organizations serving undocumented populations, this learning exchange offered an opportunity to map out strategies for influencing the immigration reform debate and educating local policy makers and opinion leaders about enforcement options that are least injurious to families and youth. Participants came from Massachusetts, Mississippi, Colorado, Texas, Washington State, and Washington, DC.

CLE Title: **Collective Leadership and Systems Change: Examining Poverty, Practice, and Policy**
Co-Hosted by: **LUPE (La Union del Pueblo Entero) and Llano Grande Center**

Location: **South Texas (San Juan and Edcouch, TX)**
Date: **April 15–18, 2010**

This learning exchange helped participants understand how systems interconnect to impact people, families, and communities. Participants were immersed in the policy issues of the South Texas border through a series of policy site visits, during which participants traveled to private homes to engage in house meetings, while others went to schools and other locations to talk about dual language programs, digital storytelling, and laws and policies that impact vulnerable children and families. They examined such issues as undocumented student access to higher education, street lights in colonias, inclusion of Cesar Chavez in history texts approved by the Texas Board of Education, and more. The process of policy was demystified as participants learned how to "disrupt the system" with their stories and experiences. Teams from Hawaii, Brooklyn, Michigan, and Texas worked on shaping their own agendas for change in their communities.

CLE Title: **Educational Equity in Rural and Urban Communities**
Co-Hosted by: **Migizi Communications of Minneapolis and New Paradigm Partners of Northern Wisconsin**
Location: **Saint Croix, U.S. Virgin Islands**
Date: **October 20–23, 2009**

Participants in this learning exchange explored how to cultivate collective leadership partnerships and create Gracious Space for work with public school systems that perpetuate disparities for different groups of students. Hosts demonstrated the importance of place and context by engaging local community activists in sharing cultural perspectives on equity including Somali, Latino, African American, and rural White identities. Participants examined challenges to educational equity that they face in their communities, shared successful approaches, and developed plans for moving past those obstacles. The exchange also highlighted the new media work of Native American youth regarding the media images of Native Americans, and the healing and forgiveness needed in communities of color.

CLE Title: **Building Strategies Across Race and Class: Forging Relationships for Social Change**
Hosted by: **Public Policy and Education Fund of New York in Buffalo, New York**
Location: **Buffalo, NY**
Date: **August 6–9, 2009**

Community change agents in this CLE learned how to incorporate proven principles of racial equity into their social change organizing efforts. This learning exchange examined the roles power and race play in creating strategies, and provided methods that community leaders can use to track their own growth as well as strategies for developing the skills of others. The Buffalo hosts were particularly skilled in translating abstract social equity intentions into concrete and actionable strategies for change. Moreover, Buffalo provided a powerful setting for this exploration, as it is home to the Erie Canal, Underground Railroad, and Colored Musicians Club—all of which are examples of how the local context has played a pivotal role in creating the current race and class dynamics in this U.S.–Canadian border town.

CLE Title: **New Mexico Community Learning Exchange**
Hosted by: **Laguna Department of Education**
Location: **Albuquerque, New Mexico vicinity**
Date: **March 17–20, 2009**

This learning exchange illuminated how the Laguna and Acoma pueblos have used storytelling to claim and maintain core identity through centuries of outside influence. The power of language, history, and the culture of place were presented as a source of collective identity and grounding for moving forward in the twenty-first century, particularly through education in the schools. Participants experienced the spirit of Acoma culture while visiting ancient Sky City, as well as the deep hospitality and generosity of the Laguna Pueblo during the feast day of St. Joseph. A strong theme of the learning exchange was the importance of working across generations to engage youths, adults, and elders in partnership.

CLE Title: **Massachusetts Community Learning**
    Exchange
Hosted by: **Roca, Inc.**
Location: **Chelsea, MA**
Date: **November 6–9, 2008**

This learning exchange showcased how Roca's Immigrant and Refugee Initiative (RIRI) has organized, partnered, and mobilized young people and adults in the community around issues of immigration, advocacy, and policy. Participants learned how to strengthen youth and adult partnerships and to use the peacemaking circles process to promote collective leadership among community change agents. They also used the arts to build relationships and engagement. The Chelsea learning exchange also spotlighted Roca's "Know Your Rights" campaign designed to help undocumented residents during a season of aggressive immigration enforcement raids that were splitting many families and communities.

CLE Title: **South Texas Community Learning Exchange**
Hosted by: **Llano Grande Center for Research and Community Development**
Location: **Edcouch and Elsa, TX**
Date: **May 15–18, 2008**

Situated in a predominantly Mexican American community on the South Texas border, this learning exchange highlighted how the Llano Grande uses youth–adult partnerships and Digital Storytelling to effect change in teaching and learning. Participants learned about the process of telling stories, analyzing stories, and constructing new stories to bring about change. Featured local projects included high school students working to persuade elected officials to clean up a toxic site in the middle of a residential area; a community group overseeing construction of new schools after passing a multi-million-dollar bond issue; and community–school partnerships in surrounding communities.

Appendix B

National Three-Day CLE Call, Theme, and Agenda

In October 2013, a local team was planning to host a Community Learning Exchange in northeast North Carolina. Historical issues have created challenges for the 14 school districts that comprise northeast North Carolina, and historical policies and practices of racial segregation have led to abject poverty. As a result, North Carolina's lowest performing schools are disproportionately clustered in this rural area. That said, northeast North Carolina has a clear and present spirit rooted in faith and family, and is marked by a resiliency and hope within families and in churches. However, why this spirit has not left the dining room tables or houses of worship and moved into community institutions like schools remains an important question.

The local CLE planning team wanted an event that would begin with acknowledging and learning about the historical trauma associated with racial segregation. The team also wanted the CLE to be a call for action—a provocation to mobilize community members around a grand challenge. The challenge was to write a new narrative of education in northeast North Carolina, a narrative built on the assets that are bountiful in the churches, schools, and homes of rural northeast North Carolina. The call for the CLE was simple:

> [to] help attendees see, reflect, and plan action for school leaders to engage in community improvement. By rejecting the myopic notions of current school reform efforts, we believe a holistic approach that engages schools and communities as one will reverse current trends. That is, we intend on learning and enacting real changes that embrace deep relationship through a love for community.

The team chose the symbol of "Sankofa" for our Community Learning Exchange. From the Akan language of Ghana, *sankofa* means "to reach back or return and get it," or more literally, "it is not taboo to go back and fetch what you forgot" (*se wo were fi na wosan kofa a yenki*). Sankofa is represented by a bird looking back, and the image reflects the meaning of Sankofa for the CLE where learning occurs first by looking back. Specifically, to move forward or advance, we first must understand our past, our roots: "Whatever we have lost, forgotten, forgone or been stripped of, can be reclaimed, revived, preserved and perpetuated" (for the meaning of *sankofa*, see http://www.duboislc.net/SankofaMeaning.html).

Leading for racial healing in schools, families and communities

**Northeast North Carolina
October 10-13, 2013**

The northeast North Carolina CLE had four guiding questions:

1. What does the story and history of North Carolina have to do with your history, and how can that guide advocacy for healing in your community?
2. What does looking back on the history of northeast North Carolina tell us about how we need to move forward?
3. What is the power source fueling this place, work, or idea?
4. What does leadership for racial healing advocacy look like?

Community LEARNING EXCHANGE
Connecting the Wisdom and Leadership of Place

WELCOME TO THE 16TH
Community Learning Exchange

IEL Institute for Educational Leadership
Leading Across Boundaries

Center for Ethical Leadership

CLE Host Team
Viola Gilbert
Larry Hodgkins
Tonya Little
Matt Militello
Liz Payne Moran
Jackson Olsen
Teicher Patterson
Karyn Pleasant
Erin Robbins
Angela Strother
Lynda Tredway
Doris Williams

CLE National Team
Cheryl Fields
Emiliano Guajardo
Francisco Guajardo
Miguel Guajardo
Chris Janson
Dominic Militello
Matt Militello
Dale Nienow
Kwesi Rollins
Steve Stapleton

Leading for racial healing in schools, families and communities

Northeast North Carolina
October 10-13, 2013

Graciously Supported By:

W.K. KELLOGG FOUNDATION

THE BAY AND PAUL FOUNDATIONS

NORTHEAST NORTH CAROLINA CLE
www.northcarolinacle.org

NE CLE GR

Franklinton Center at Bricks
261 Bricks Lane
Whitakers, NC 27891

The Northeast North Carolina Community Learning Exchange Program

THURSDAY, OCTOBER 10
Coming to Know Place and Space

Time	Activity	Place
1-5:00p	Arrival	Shuttles from RDU to Franklinton Center	
3-5:00p	Registration	Main Building
5-6:00p	Structured Team Conversations	Outside
	Exploring Franklinton Center at Bricks	
	History of Bricks	Old School House
6:00p	Dinner and Welcome	Café
	Entertainment: The Abbotts	
	Transition Break	
7:45p	Opening Circle	Main Meeting Room
	Team Shirts and Individual Sharing	

FRIDAY, OCTOBER 11
Looking Back
"It is not taboo to reach back and fetch what you forgot." ~Sankofa

Time	Activity	Place
7:00a	Breakfast	Café
8:00a	Depart for Site Visits	Main Building
1:00p	Group Photo	Outside
1:15p	Play	Folk Life	
	Double Dutch, Praise Dancing, Freedom/Civil Rights Songs, and Volleyball	Outside
2:30p	Play Cool Down and Home Team Learning Walk	Any Open Space
	Transition Break (Find Your Affinity Group Station)	
4:00p	Meet in Affinity Groups: School Leaders, University Faculty, Community Members, and Youth	Any Open Space
5-6:00p	Artistic Expressions of Site Visits by Affinity Groups	Main Meeting Room
	Hosting a CLE Reflection: The North Florida Story	
	Transition Break	
6:15p	Traditional Southern Fish Fry	Café
7:30p	Reflections	Open Space for Conversations	
	Fireside Stories and Smores	Any Open Space
	Video Game Room	

SATURDAY, OCTOBER 12
Healing and Moving Forward
"Gather the best of what our past has to teach us, so that we can achieve our full potential as we move forward." ~Sankofa

Time	Activity	Place
7:30a	Breakfast	Café
8:30a	Facilitating Conversations of Race and Equity: Advocacy for Racial Healing	
9:30a	CLE Pedagogies: Open Space World Café Circle, Gracious Space, Site Visits, Meaningful Conversations, Folk Life/Play, Theme & Guiding Questions, Evaluation, & Digital Presence	Main Meeting Room
10:30a	Hosting a CLE Reflection: The Halifax Story	
	Transition Break	
11:15a	Team Time: CLE in your own context	Any Open Space
12:00p	Lunch	Café
	Team Time Continued	
1-4:00p	Gallery Walk and Critical Friends	Any Open Space
	Team's Refine Plans	
	Transition Break	
4:30p	Closing Circle	Main Meeting Room
6:30p	Traditional Southern BBQ Entertainment: Edgecombe County HS Gospel Choir Open Mic Reflections & Performances Check Out Logistics	Shuttles to RDU	Café

SUNDAY, OCTOBER 13
Leaving to Begin

Time	Activity	Place
4a-10a	Departures	Shuttles to RDU	Outside Main Building
7:00a	Breakfast	Café

The Northeast North Carolina Community Learning Exchange Agenda

Appendix C

One-Day CLE (Embedded in a University-Based Course)

Collective Leadership and Family: What We Learn About Leadership From Our Families—and How We Can Use Those Learnings to Engage Other Families

> EDA 7192: Leadership in the Group Context
> University of North Florida
> Murray Hill Christ Community Church
> April 6, 2013

Introductions, Appreciations, and Commitments (9:00–9:40)

- *Travis Pinckney, Jeff Will, & Chris Janson*

Musical Performance (9:40–9:50)

- *Travis Pinckney, Jeffrey Will, & Guests*

Moving Beyond Barriers: Leadership & Education Centered on Family Needs (9:50–10:00)

Exchange Sessions, Round 1 (10:00–11:00)

Session Host(s)	Topic
Jeff Will, Phoenix Cooper, D'Angelo Williams & guests	Youth Voice, Leadership, and Family
Bob Janson	Using Collective Leadership: Engaging Families From a Public School District Level
Marvin Brown & Gregory Curry	Re-envisioning Family Engagement and Empowerment at the School Building Level
UNF Educational Leadership Doctoral Students	Digital Story Showcase: Self as Leader

Exchange Sessions, Round 2 (11:00–12:00)

Session Host(s)	Topic
Saponda Allen & Umesheka McNeil	Re-framing Family Conversations to Better Support Youth College Aspirations
Bob Janson	Using Collective Leadership Engaging Families From a Public School District Level
Giovanni Haertel	Creating Cultures of Support for and Among Sexual Minority Youth and Their Families
UNF Educational Leadership Doctoral Students	Digital Story Showcase: Self as Leader

LUNCH—Tremendous BBQ (12:00–12:30)

• Minister Anthony Moore

Exchange Sessions, Round 3 (12:30–1:30)

Session Host(s)	Topic
Travis Pinckey	Arts, Life, and Beats: The Role of Music in Family and Community Leadership
Jeff Will	Youth Voice, Leadership, and Family
Giovanni Haertel	Creating Cultures of Support for and Among Sexual Minority Youth and Their Families
UNF Educational Leadership Doctoral Students	Digital Story Showcase: Self as Leader
Minister Anthony Moore	Faith-Based Impact on Family and Family Culture

Sharing Meaning From Exchanges (1:30–2:30)

Closing Circle (2:30–3:30)

• Travis Pinckney

"So . . . what are YOU going to do when you get back home?"

Appendix D
Family Wisdom Exchange

Ribault HS Student Wisdom Exchange
GEAR UP—University of North Florida SOAR
Tuesday, April 15, 2014
Take the Stage!!!
Looking Back to Look Forward

Opening Circle, Framing the Evening: Looking Back at Our Time

- As the result of GEAR UP mentoring:

    - Students: How have you grown? What have you noticed about yourself
      that is different?
    - Caregivers/Parents: How has your student grown? What have you
      noticed about him/her that is different now?
    - Mentors: How have you grown? How are you a better educator/counselor?

Session 1 Exchanges

Please find the session that best fits your needs and/or interests

---

Minute to Win It—Recreation and play as a
community building tool

Avoiding Summer Melt—Each year, 10%–
20% of all college-eligible or enrolled
students never attend. This session will
include conversation focusing on how to
avoid this.

Preparing for College Life—This session
will include discussion around those
things that are needed for a transition to
college life, such as what to bring, how
to develop supportive relationships, and
how to get ready for roommates.

*College Decision-Making and
Planning*—Considerations for making
college choices

Last Minute College Planning—This session
focuses on college transition planning for
those who only recently decided they
want to go to college.

Other—This spot is open for new topics
from any of the participants.

Session 2 Exchanges (time permitting)

Please find the session that best fits your needs and/or interests

---

Minute to Win It—Recreation and play as a community building tool

Avoiding Summer Melt—Each year, 10%–20% of all college-eligible or enrolled students never attend. This session will include conversation focusing on how to avoid this.

Preparing for College Life—This session will include discussion around those things that are needed for a transition to college life, such as what to bring, how to develop supportive relationships, and how to get ready for roommates.

College Decision-Making and Planning—Considerations for making college choices

Last Minute College Planning—This session focuses on college transition planning for those who only recently decided they want to go to college.

Other—This spot is open for new topics from any of the participants.

Closing Thoughts and Reflections

Appendix E

Photo and Video Release Form

I hereby grant permission to the rights of my image, likeness, and sound of my voice as recorded on audio or video tape without payment or any other consideration as part of the work of the Community Learning Exchange. I understand that my image may be edited, copied, exhibited, published, or distributed and waive the right to inspect or approve the finished product wherein my likeness appears. Additionally, I waive any right to royalties or other compensation arising or related to the use of my image or recording. I also understand that this material may be used in diverse educational settings within an unrestricted geographic area.

Photographic, audio or video recordings may be used for the following purposes:

- conference presentations
- educational presentations or courses
- informational presentations
- on-line educational courses
- on-line/off-line promotional material
- evaluation needs related to the gatherings

By signing this release I understand this permission signifies that photographic or video recordings of me may be electronically displayed via the Internet or in the public educational setting.

I will be consulted about the use of the photographs or video recording for any purpose other than those listed above. There is no time limit on the validity of this release nor is there any geographic limitation on where these materials may be distributed. This release applies to photographic, audio or video recordings collected as part of the gathering in which I am currently attending.

By signing this form I acknowledge that I have completely read and fully understand the above release and agree to be bound thereby. I hereby release any and all claims against any person or organization utilizing this material for educational purposes.

Full Name _____

Street Address/P.O. Box _____

City/State _____ Zip Code _____

Phone _____ Email Address _____

Signature _____ Date _____

If this release is obtained from a participant under the age of 18, then the signature of the sponsor is also required.

Sponsor Signature _____ Date _____

ADDITIONAL RESOURCES

Readings

Ecology of Self

Coelho, P. (1995). *The alchemist*. San Francisco, CA: Harper.

Guajardo, M., & Guajardo, F. (2008). Two brothers in higher education: Weaving a social fabric for service in academic—A model of interdependence. In R. Padilla & K. Gonzalez (Eds.), *Latino perspectives on higher education for the public good: An intergenerational approach* (pp. 60–81). Herndon, VA: Stylus.

Guajardo, F., Guajardo, M., Oliver, J., Valadez, M., & Cantu, M. (2013). Digital storytelling for critical reflection: An educational leadership story. In M. Militello & J. Friend (Eds.), *Principal 2.0: Technology and educational leadership* (pp. 149–171). Charlotte, NC: Information Age.

Guajardo, M.A., Oliver, J., Rodríguez, G., Valadez, M., Cantu, Y., & Guajardo, F.J. (2011). Reframing the praxis of school leadership preparation through digital storytelling. *Journal of Research on Leadership Education, 6*(5), 145–161.

Habermas, J. (1984). *The theory of communicative action* (Vol. 2, T. McCarthy, Trans.). Boston, MA: Beacon Press.

Schon, D. (1983). *The reflective practitioner*. New York, NY: Basic Books.

Steele, C. (2011). *Whistling Vivaldi: How stereotypes affect us and what we can do*. New York, NY: W.W. Norton.

Ecology of Organization

Argyris, C. (1992). *On organizational learning*. Cambridge, MA: Blackwell Business.

Bowles, S., & Gintis, H. (1976). *Schooling in a capitalistic America: Educational reform and the contradictions of economic life*. New York, NY: Basic Books.

DiMaggio, P.J., & Powell, W.W. (1991). The iron cage revisited: Institutional isomorphism and collective rationality in organizational fields. In W.W. Powell & P.J. DiMaggio (Eds.), *The new institutionalism in organizational analysis* (pp. 63–82). Chicago, IL: University of Chicago Press.

Guajardo, M.A., Beaty, D., & Guajardo, F.J. (2005). Parental involvement and engagement: History and examples from two Hispanic schools. In A. Pankake, M. Littleton, &

G. Schroth (Eds.), *The administration and supervision of special programs in education* (2nd ed., pp. 225–235). Dubuque, IA: Kendall/Hunt.

March, J.G. (1988). The technology of foolishness. In J.G. March (Ed.), *Decisions and organizations* (pp. 253–265). New York, NY: Basil Blackwell.

March, J.G. (1999). Exploration and exploitation in organizational learning. In J.G. March (Ed.), *The pursuit of organizational intelligence* (pp. 114–136). Malden, MA: Blackwell.

Militello, M., & Janson, C. (2015). *InQuiry: Finally an evaluation methodology of the people, for the people.* Unpublished manuscript.

Putnam, R.D. (2015). *Our kids: The American dream in crisis.* New York, NY: Simon & Schuster.

Rawls, J. (1971). *A theory of justice.* Cambridge, MA: Harvard University Press.

Sergiovanni, T. (2000). *The lifeworld of leadership: Creating culture, community and personal meaning in our schools.* San Francisco, CA: Jossey-Bass.

Weick, K. (1995). *Sensemaking in organizations.* Thousand Oaks, CA: Sage.

Ecology of Community

Alinsky, S. (1969). *Reveille for radicals.* New York, NY: Vintage Books.

Block, P. (2009). *Community: The structure of belonging.* San Francisco, CA: Berrett-Koehler.

Guajardo, M. (2009). Collective leadership: Practice, theory, and praxis. *Journal of Leadership Studies, 3*(2), 70–73.

Guajardo, M., & Guajardo, F. (2002). Critical ethnography and community change. In Y. Zou & H. Trueba (Eds.), *Ethnography and schools: Qualitative approaches to the study of education* (pp. 281–304). Lanham, MD: Rowman & Littlefield.

Guajardo, M., & Guajardo, F. (2010). Social advocacy and community change: Relationships, resistance, and revolution. In M. Benham, D. Nienow, K. Ruder, & M. Militello (Eds.), *Kellogg leadership for community change: Crossing boundaries, strengthening communities* (pp. 34–42). Lawrence, KS: Allen Press.

Guajardo, F., Perez, D., Ozuna, J., Guajardo, M., Davila, E., & Casaperalta, N. (2006). Youth voice and the Llano Grande Center. *International Journal of Leadership in Education, 9*(4), 359.

Militello, M., Janson, C., Guajardo, E., & Militello, D. (2014). *Community Learning Exchange annual report.* Washington, DC: Institute for Educational Leadership.

Putnam, R.D. (2000). *Bowling alone: The collapse and revival of American community.* New York, NY: Touchstone.

Rice, D. (2001). *Crazy loco.* New York, NY: Dial Books.

Ruder, K., Nienow, D., Guajardo, E., Guajardo, M., & Fields, C. (Eds.). (2010). *Weaving strong communities: The collective leadership storybook.* Seattle, WA: Center for Ethical Leadership.

Wenger, E. (1998). *Communities of practice: Learning, meaning and identity.* Cambridge, MA: Cambridge University Press.

Axiom: Learning and Leadership Are Dynamic Social Processes

Benham, M. (2002). An alternative perspective of educational leadership for change: Reflections on Native/Indigenous ways of knowing. In K. Leithwood & P. Hallinger (Eds.), *Second international handbook of educational leadership and administration* (pp. 133–165). Dordrecht, Holland: Kluwer Academic.

Benham, M., Militello, M., & Ruder, K. (2010). Learning and living—into collective leadership. In M. Benham, D. Nienow, K. Ruder, & M. Militello (Eds.), *Kellogg leadership for community change: Crossing boundaries, strengthening communities* (pp. 9–21). Lawrence, KS: Allen Press.

Labaree, D. (1999). *How to succeed in school without really learning.* New Haven, CT: Yale University Press.

Militello, M., & Benham, M. (2010). "Sorting out" collective leadership: How Q-methodology can be used to evaluate leadership development. *Leadership Quarterly, 21*(4), 620–632.

Militello, M., Rallis, S.F., & Goldring, E.B. (2009). *Leading with inquiry and action: How principals improve teaching and learning.* Thousand Oaks, CA: Corwin Press.

Wheatley, M.J. (2007). Leadership of self-organized networks: Lessons from the war on terror. *Performance Improvement Quarterly, 20*(2), 59–66.

Axiom: Conversations Are Critical and Central Pedagogical Processes

Brown, J., & Isaacs, D. (2005). *The World Café: Shaping our futures through conversations that matter.* San Francisco, CA: Berrett-Koehler.

Freedman, J., & Combs, G. (1996). *Narrative therapy: The social construction of preferred realities.* New York, NY: W.W. Norton.

Ganz, M. (2011). Public narrative, collective action, and power. In S. Odugbemi & T. Lee (Eds.), *Accountability through public opinion: From inertia to public action* (pp. 269–286). Washington, DC: The World Bank.

Grimaldo, L., & Guajardo, M.A. (in press). Images and practices of deficit thinking: Embracing story for civic engagement. *Cuadernos interdisciplinarios pedagógicos.*

Guajardo, F., & Guajardo, M. (2013). The power of Platica. *Reflections: A Journal of Public Rhetoric, Civic Writing, and Service Learning, 13*(1), 159–164.

Haberman, M. (1991). The pedagogy of poverty versus good teaching. *Phi Delta Kappan, 73*(4), 290–294.

Hughes, P., & Grace, B. (2010). *Gracious Space: A practical guide to working together* (2nd ed.). Seattle, WA: Center for Ethical Leadership.

Janson, C., Parikh, S., Young, J., & Fudge, L. (2011). Constructing collective understanding in school: Principal and student use of Iterative Digital Reflection. *Journal of Research on Leadership Education, 11*(6), 162–180.

Wheatley, M.J. (2009). *Turning to one another: Simple conversations to restore hope to the future* (2nd ed.). San Francisco, CA: Berrett-Koehler.

Axiom: The People Closest to the Issues Are Best Situated to Discover Answers to the Local Concerns

Adams, F., & Horton, M. (1975). *Unearthing the seeds of fire: The idea of Highlander.* Winston-Salem, NC: John F. Blair.

Addams, J. (1938). *Twenty years at Hull House: With autobiographical notes.* New York, NY: Macmillan.

Brown, S. (2006). A match made in heaven: A marginalized methodology for studying the marginalized. *Quality & Quantity, 40,* 361–382.

Dewey, J. (1963). *Experience and education.* New York, NY: Collier Books.

Freire, P. (1997). *Pedagogy of the oppressed.* New York, NY: Continuum.

Gaventa, J. (1980). *Power and powerlessness: Quiescence and rebellion in an Appalachian valley.* Chicago, IL: University of Illinois Press.

Horton, M., Freire, P., Bell, B., Gaventa, J., & Peters, J. (1990). *We make the road by walking: Conversations on education and social change.* Philadelphia, PA: Temple University Press.

Horton, M., & Jacobs, D. (2003). *The Myles Horton reader: Education for social change.* Knoxville, TN: University of Tennessee Press.

Horton, M., Kohl, J., & Kohl, H. (1990). *The long haul: An autobiography.* New York, NY: Teachers College Press.

Kretzmann, J., & McKnight, J. (1993). *Building communities from the inside out: Path toward finding and mobilizing a community's assets*. Chicago, IL: ACTA.

Smith, L.T. (1999). *Decolonizing methodologies: Research and indigenous peoples*. New York, NY: Zed Books.

Axiom: Crossing Boundaries Enriches the Developmental and Educational Process

Giroux, H.S. (1992). *Border crossings: Cultural workers and the politics of education*. New York, NY: Routledge

Guajardo, F., Guajardo, M., Oliver, J., & Keawe, L. (2012). Framework for a new political praxis: Respeto, dignidad, y conocimiento. *Journal of the Association of Mexican American Educators, 6*(1), 52–60.

Homans, G. (1950). *The human group*. New York, NY: Harcourt, Brace.

Hooks, B. (1994). *Outlaw culture: Resisting representations*. London, England: Routledge.

Militello, M., Militello, D., Militello, L., Militello, G., & Militello, R. (2013). Technology and education: An intergenerational reflection and prognostication. In M. Militello & J. Friend (Eds.), *Principal 2.0: Technology and educational leadership* (pp. 51–63). Charlotte, NC: Information Age.

Vygotsky, L.S. (1962). *Thought and language*. Cambridge, MA: MIT Press.

Axiom: Hope and Change Are Built on Assets and Dreams of Locals and Their Communities

Guajardo, F., Alvarez, S., Guajardo, M., Garcia, S., Guajardo, J. A., & Marquez, J. (2014). Braceros, Mexicans, Americans, and schools: (Re) imagining teaching and learning in Mexican America. *Rio Bravo Journal, 23*(1), 9–41.

Jacobs, D. (2003). *The Myles Horton reader: Education for social change*. Knoxville: University of Tennessee Press.

Jones, M.H. (2004). *The autobiography of Mother Jones*. Mineola, NY: Dover.

McKnight, J., & Block, P. (2010). *The abundant community: Awakening the power of families and neighborhoods*. San Francisco, CA: Berrett-Koehler.

Theory of Change

Benham, M. (Ed.). (2008). *Indigenous educational models for contemporary practice: In our mother's voice II*. New York, NY: Routledge.

Friend, J., & Militello, M. (2015). Lights, camera, action! Advancing learning, research, and service through video production in educational leadership preparation. *Journal of Research on Leadership Education*, Online First. Available at http://jrl.sagepub.com/content/early/2014/12/14/1942775114561120.full.pdf+html.

Guajardo, M., & Guajardo, F. (2004). The impact of Brown on the Brown of South Texas: A micropolitical perspective on the education of Mexican Americans in a rural South Texas community. *American Educational Research Journal, 41*(3), 501–526.

Guajardo, F., & Guajardo, M. (2010). Cultivating stories of change. In K. Ruder (Ed.), *Weaving strong communities: The collective leadership storybook* (pp. 85–103). Seattle, WA: Center for Ethical Leadership.

Guajardo, M., Guajardo, F., & Casaperalta, E. (2008). Transformative education: Chronicling a pedagogy for social change. *Anthropology and Education Quarterly, 39*(1), 3–22.

Guajardo, F., Guajardo, M., Oliver, J., & Keawe, L. (2012). Framework for a new political praxis: Respeto, dignidad, y conocimiento. *Journal of the Association of Mexican American Educators, 6*(1), 52–60.

Hoggan, C., & Militello, M. (2015). Digital stories to promote reflection and community in doctoral education. *Journal of Continuing Higher Education, 63*(2), 119–125.

Marris, P. (1974). *Loss and change.* New York, NY: Pantheon Books.

Militello, M., & Friend, J. (Eds.). (2013). *Principal 2.0: Technology and educational leadership.* Charlotte, NC: Information Age.

Militello, M., & Guajardo, F. (2013). Virtually speaking: How digital storytelling can facilitate organizational learning. *Journal of Community Positive Practices, 13*(2), 80–91.

Rogers, E. (2003). *Diffusion of innovation* (5th ed.). New York, NY: Free Press.

Surowiecki, J. (2005). *Wisdom of crowds.* New York, NY: Anchor Books.

Warren, M. (2001). *Dry bones rattling: Community building to revitalize American democracy.* Princeton, NJ: Princeton University Press.

Weissglass, J. (1990). Constructivist listening for empowerment and change. *The Educational Forum, 50*(4), 351–370.

Web Links

Institute for Educational Leadership
www.iel.org

Llano Grande Center
www.llanogrande.org

Leadership Learning Exchange
http://www.ecu.edu/cs-acad/dcs/LearningExchange.cfm

Community Learning Exchange
www.communitylearningexchange.org

Kellogg Foundation
www.wkkf.org

Highlander Center
www.highlandercenter.org

Center for Ethical Leadership
www.ethicalleadership.org

EduTrope (InQuiry)
www.edutrope.com

The Asset-Based Community Development Institute and Mapping Resources
www.abcdinstitute.org
www.abcdinstitute.org/docs/MappingCapacity.pdf

North Dakota Study Group
www.ndsg.org

The World Café
www.theworldcafe.com

Rural School and Community Trust
www.ruraledu.org

Institute for Educational Leadership
www.iel.org

University Council for Educational Administration (UCEA)
  Modules
http://ucealee.squarespace.com/neighborhood-walk-ple

Video Links

Book Poem
http://vimeo.com/edutrope/leefrancis

Place/CLE Host Site
www.ucc.org/franklinton-center

Llano Grande Center

Llano Grade Overview I	http://vimeo.com/edutrope/llanogrande
Llano Grande Overview II	http://vimeo.com/edutrope/llanograndeoverview
History of Llano Grande Center	http://vimeo.com/edutrope/lgbeginnings
Myrta's Personal Digital Story	http://vimeo.com/edutrope/myrta
Red Barn Project	http://vimeo.com/edutrope/redbarn
Story of the Llano Grande House	http://vimeo.com/edutrope/lghouse
Impact of the Llano Grande Center	http://vimeo.com/edutrope/llanograndealumni

CLE Pedagogies
Circle
  Collective Leadership: http://vimeo.com/edutrope/collectiveleadership

Community Site Visits
  Economic Rebirth: http://vimeo.com/edutrope/rockymount
  Historic Downtown: http://vimeo.com/edutrope/halifax

Civil Rights Movement: http://vimeo.com/edutrope/Williamston
Remnants of an Unresolved Murder: http://vimeo.com/edutrope/oxford
Organic Farm: http://vimeo.com/edutrope/mao

Community Mapping

Module: http://vimeo.com/edutrope/moduleiv
Brooklyn CLE: http://vimeo.com/edutrope/brooklyn

Digital Engagement

Highlights from the Washington, DC CLE: http://vimeo.com/edutrope/dco-pening
Reflections on a CLE in Honolulu, HI: http://vimeo.com/edutrope/clereflections
Reflections on Engagement from the Seattle, WA CLE: http://vimeo.com/edutrope/cleseattle
Bringing Learning from CLE Back Home: http://vimeo.com/edutrope/clemontana
What is your recipe for change? http://vimeo.com/edutrope/recipe
What is your gift? http://vimeo.com/edutrope/clegift
Youth Voices: http://vimeo.com/edutrope/youthvoice

InQuiry

InQuiry Process: http://vimeo.com/edutrope/qintro and http://vimeo.com/edutrope/inquiryprocess
InQuiry Sharing:http://vimeo.com/edutrope/qseattle and http://vimeo.com/edutrope/qreporting
Gift of the Bitterroot: http://vimeo.com/edutrope/giftofthebitterroot

Learning Walk

Jacksonville CLE: http://vimeo.com/edutrope/communitywalk
Leadership Learning Exchange: http://vimeo.com/edutrope/eppeslearningxchange

Meaningful Conversations

*Meaningful Conversations on Education:*http://vimeo.com/edutrope/educationnarrative

Performance

Open Mic Night: http://vimeo.com/edutrope/centraltexas
CLE Theme Song: http://vimeo.com/edutrope/courage
CLE Participant Reflection Poem: http://vimeo.com/edutrope/reflectionpoem

Digital Stories, Self-as-Leader

Darren: http://vimeo.com/edutrope/darren
Tonya: http://vimeo.com/edutrope/tonya
Karyn: http://vimeo.com/edutrope/karyn

Appendix

One-Day CLEs
South Creek Middle School: http://vimeo.com/edutrope/onedaycle

Family Wisdom Exchanges
Ribault High School: http://vimeo.com/edutrope/rhs
Jackson High School: http://vimeo.com/edutrope/jhs

ABOUT THE AUTHORS

Miguel A. Guajardo is an associate professor in the Education and Community Leadership Program and a member of the doctoral faculty in the School Improvement at Texas State University. He joined Texas State University in 2004. His research interests include issues of community building, community youth development, leadership development, race and ethnicity, university and community partnerships, and Latino youth and families. Guajardo was a Fellow with the Kellogg International Leadership Program and the Salzburg Seminar. He is also a co-founder and the chairman of the board of directors of the Llano Grande Center for Research and Development, an education and community youth development organization in South Texas.

Francisco Guajardo is professor and C. Bascom Slemp Endowed Chair in Education at the University of Texas, Rio Grande Valley. He is a founder of the Llano Grande Center for Research and Development, based in Edcouch-Elsa High School (HS) in rural South Texas, and a founding member of the Center for Bilingual Studies at UT Pan American, a center working to shape the new University of Texas, Rio Grande Valley as a bilingual university. Born in Rio Bravo in Tamaulipas, Mexico, he immigrated with his family to South Texas and became part of the migrant farm working stream: first traveling to Keeler, Michigan, then to Buttonwillow in the San Joaquin Valley in California; Hereford, in the Texas Panhandle; and in and around the agricultural fields of the Rio Grande Valley. After graduating from Edcouch-Elsa HS, he earned a bachelor's degree in English, a master's degree in history, and a PhD in educational leadership from the University of Texas at Austin. As a professor of educational leadership and through his work with Llano Grande, he has worked in more than 35 states in the United States, and internationally in countries such as Austria, Italy, Sweden, England, New Zealand, Peru, Mexico, and Canada.

Christopher Janson is an associate professor in the Department of Leadership, School Counseling, and Sport Management at the University of North Florida, where he teaches both school counseling and educational leadership courses. His scholarship has resulted in more than 20 publications centered on research interests including school counselor skill and dispositional development, inter-professional relationships in schools, educational leadership, urban education, and transformative pedagogy. Janson is a program developer for a university-community school grant partnership focused on increasing career and college readiness for students in urban schools, and he is also involved with a community initiative to raise awareness and elicit support in challenging the community's persisting high dropout rate.

Matthew Militello is the Wells Fargo Distinguished Professor in Educational Leadership at East Carolina University. He has previously held faculty positions at North Carolina State University (2008–2014) and the University of Massachusetts at Amherst (2005–2008). Prior to his academic career, Militello was a middle and high public school teacher, assistant principal, and principal in Michigan (1992–2003). Militello has more than 50 publications, including more than 30 peer-refereed articles and four other books: *Leading With Inquiry and Action: How Principals Improve Teaching and Learning* (Corwin Press, 2009); *Principals Teaching the Law: 10 Legal Lessons Your Teachers Must Know* (Corwin Press, 2010); *Principal 2.0: Technology and Educational Leadership* (Information Age, 2013); and *How to Prevent Special Education Litigation: Eight Legal Lesson Plans* (Teachers College Press, 2015). Militello has received funding to conduct research from the College Board, the Commonwealth of Massachusetts, the W.K. Kellogg Foundation, and Xian Normal University, as well as a multi-million-dollar Race to the Top grant to train school leaders in northeast North Carolina. He has also evaluated projects for the National Science Foundation and the U.S. Department of Education.

★ ★ ★ ★ ★ ★

Growing up together in South Texas, Miguel and Francisco learned and lived the community with their family. Matt and Chris met in 2001 when Matt, a high school administrator, hired Chris as a school counselor; their Community Learning Exchange journey began with their professional work in that public school and has continued since within diverse universities, organizations, and communities. Today, the four work with colleagues, communities, and institutions across the country promoting the spirit, importance, and effectiveness of the Community

Learning Exchange, with the goal of helping others begin growing the work within their own organizations and communities. Together, they teach and learn from friends old and new, which in turn continually shapes the exchange as the work is informed by the wisdom and gifts of each new group of CLE participants and their communities.

INDEX

Note: page numbers in italics indicate illustrations.